Microsoft Office
POWERPOINT 2007
Complete Makeover Kit

Geetesh Bajaj
Echo Swinford

800 East 96th Street, Indianapolis, Indiana 46240 USA

Microsoft® Office PowerPoint® 2007 Complete Makeover Kit

ISBN-13: 978-0-7897-3681-9
ISBN-10: 0-7897-3681-0

Cheshire, Jim.
  The Expression Web developer's guide to ASP.NET 3.5 : learn to create ASP.NET applications using Visual Web Developer 2008 / Jim Cheshire.
    p. cm.
  Includes index.
  ISBN 0-7897-3665-9
  1. Active server pages. 2. Web site development. 3. Web sites—Authoring programs. 4. Microsoft Expression Web. I. Title.
  TK5105.8885.A26C458 2008
  006.7'6—dc22
                    2007039133

Printed in the United States of America
Second Printing: March 2008

Trademarks

All terms mentioned in this book that are known to be trademarks or service marks have been appropriately capitalized. Que Publishing cannot attest to the accuracy of this information. Use of a term in this book should not be regarded as affecting the validity of any trademark or service mark.

Microsoft and PowerPoint are registered trademarks of Microsoft Corporation.

Warning and Disclaimer

Every effort has been made to make this book as complete and as accurate as possible, but no warranty or fitness is implied. The information provided is on an "as is" basis. The authors and the publisher shall have neither liability nor responsibility to any person or entity with respect to any loss or damages arising from the information contained in this book or from the use of the CD or programs accompanying it.

Bulk Sales

Que Publishing offers excellent discounts on this book when ordered in quantity for bulk purchases or special sales. For more information, please contact

> **U.S. Corporate and Government Sales**
> **1-800-382-3419**
> **corpsales@pearsontechgroup.com**

For sales outside the United States, please contact

> **International Sales**
> **international@pearsoned.com**

This Book Is Safari Enabled

The Safari® Enabled icon on the cover of your favorite technology book means the book is available through Safari Bookshelf. When you buy this book, you get free access to the online edition for 45 days.

Safari Bookshelf is an electronic reference library that lets you easily search thousands of technical books, find code samples, download chapters, and access technical information whenever and wherever you need it.

To gain 45-day Safari Enabled access to this book:

- Go to http://www.quepublishing.com/safarienabled
- Complete the brief registration form
- Enter the coupon code FYGG-LXDF-TT2Y-1LF2-MKQ1

If you have difficulty registering on Safari Bookshelf or accessing the online edition, please email customer-service@safaribooksonline.com.

Associate Publisher
Greg Wiegand

Acquisitions Editor
Loretta Yates

Development Editor
Laura Norman

Managing Editor
Patrick Kanouse

Senior Project Editor
Tonya Simpson

Copy Editor
Jill Batistick

Indexer
Ken Johnson

Proofreader
Elizabeth Scott

Technical Editor
Julie Terberg

Publishing Coordinator
Cindy Teeters

Multimedia Developer
Dan Scherf

Book Designer
Anne Jones

Composition
Bronkella Publishing

CONTENTS AT A GLANCE

TABLE OF CONTENTS

ON THE CD

About the Authors

Geetesh Bajaj has been a Microsoft PowerPoint MVP since 2001. He heads a presentation design studio based in India, where he lives with his wife and two children.

Geetesh has authored two books published by Wiley: *Cutting Edge PowerPoint For Dummies* and *Cutting Edge PowerPoint 2007 For Dummies*. He also co-authored a book published by Que: *Special Edition Using Microsoft Office PowerPoint 2007*.

Although Geetesh loves to write articles, design PowerPoint templates, and update his dozen-odd websites, his most enjoyable task is to take ugly presentations and make them look wow. That's how the idea of this book originated.

You can sign up for his newsletter at www.indezine.com.

From 1997 through August 2005, **Echo Swinford** worked for a medical education communications company, where she was responsible for the development of enduring materials and standalone modules for continuing medical education programs. She recently completed her master's degree in New Media at the Indiana University-Purdue University at Indianapolis School of Informatics and works as a self-employed presentation specialist.

Echo's first book, *Fixing PowerPoint Annoyances*, was published by O'Reilly Media in February 2006, and she has a string of technical editing credits with other publishers. Echo has been a Microsoft PowerPoint MVP since early 2000. You can find PowerPoint tips and tricks on her website, www.echosvoice.com.

A Word from the Authors: We wanted to do a book together for a long time, but other book projects kept getting in the way. We're sure you'll find it was worth the wait!

Dedication

We dedicate this book to outstanding PowerPoint presentations!

Acknowledgments

A book can never be a singular achievement because it takes the effort of so many people to bring you what you are reading now. A number of people made the writing of this book possible.

We wish to thank the universal power that enlivens all of us, and our families.

We'd like to thank Stephanie McComb for getting us started on the right track and give a huge shout-out to Loretta Yates for her patience and for finishing things up right! Laura Norman's know-how was invaluable. Tonya Simpson, Dan Scherf, Jill Batistick, and the entire team at Que were patient and awesome.

Thanks to Richard Bretschneider, Howard Cooperstein, John Langhans, April Spence, and Abhishek Kant at Microsoft.

Julie Terberg's technical expertise and fantastic design sense were huge contributions.

We're very grateful for everyone's input, including names we might have forgotten.

We Want to Hear from You!

As the reader of this book, *you* are our most important critic and commentator. We value your opinion and want to know what we're doing right, what we could do better, what areas you'd like to see us publish in, and any other words of wisdom you're willing to pass our way.

As an associate publisher for Que Publishing, I welcome your comments. You can email or write me directly to let me know what you did or didn't like about this book, as well as what we can do to make our books better.

Please note that I cannot help you with technical problems related to the topic of this book. We do have a User Services group, however, where I will forward specific technical questions related to the book.

When you write, please be sure to include this book's title and authors as well as your name, email address, and phone number. I will carefully review your comments and share them with the authors and editors who worked on the book.

Email: feedback@quepublishing.com

Mail: Greg Wiegand
Associate Publisher
Que Publishing
800 East 96th Street
Indianapolis, IN 46240 USA

Reader Services

Visit our website and register this book at www.quepublishing.com/register for convenient access to any updates, downloads, or errata that might be available for this book.

Also, check out the book's companion site at www.pptkit.com/.

This book is all about remaking your PowerPoint presentations so that they look better and you become more successful. Consider this question: Is this book old wine packaged in a new bottle? Read the question again: Old wine packaged in a new bottle.

Now choose one word that you consider to be the most important within the question, and tell us why you chose that particular word. Because we can't personally ask all our readers this question, we did the next best thing: We asked our friends! In addition, to be absolutely sure that the results would not be overly influenced by our friends, we also asked this question in a private online forum populated by people whom we had never met.

Here's our analysis of their responses:

- If you chose **old**, you probably have tons of PowerPoint files from years and years of creating and delivering presentations. This book will help you make those presentations look more contemporary and stylish.

- If you chose **wine**, you like the finer things in life—the bottles themselves don't matter as much to you. Fine presentation design is an art form that will become familiar to you within the covers of this book.

- If you chose **new**, you probably are a novice—or at least someone who loves to learn new things all the time. You will enjoy the tricks you will learn in this book.

- If you chose **bottle**, you are open to options and are brave. Very few people admitted that their first choice of a word in this phrase was bottle. Brave people love to break rules, as you'll learn in this book.

- But what if you chose **packaged**, or why did you *not* choose that word? Well, the book you are holding in your hands is all about packaging. It doesn't matter whether the wine is old or the bottle is new. What's important is the packaging, because if the packaging doesn't give you sufficient information in a way that's pleasing to you, you might never even try the wine!

Yes, that was just an analogy; after all, one of the authors of this book doesn't even drink wine!

The PowerPoint presentation that you create or make over is packaging. Packaging is very important; in fact, let us repeat this and say it again: It is the packaging that will attract the potential client, possible investor, or perceived respondent, and the makeovers in this book will help you create better packaging.

If someone tells you that packaging is not important, ask him to compare a Cadillac to a Yugo. (After all, they both run, but which would you prefer to look at?) Or ask him if he's ever noticed how the food in a five-star restaurant is presented, how light falls on a solitaire diamond in a jewelry store, how some television commercials are better than others, or how people all over the world decorate their homes on holidays. The world expects great packaging, and our world has moved so far forward in the last few years that anything not properly packaged is hardly given a second glance. That might not be a great state of affairs, but then, we are not out to change the world; we just want to make your PowerPoint presentations look better!

Why We Wrote This Book

We wrote this book because we wanted to share what we have learned over the years. We wanted to use those ideas to bring alive countless presentations all over the world so that the perception of "dead PowerPoint" dies.

There probably are 30 million PowerPoint users out there who can choose from a gazillion PowerPoint books that attempt to be replacements for manuals or to go a little further and show users how they can use the tons of features PowerPoint provides. Those books are more like reference books that can be pulled off the bookshelf when required. This book is not a replacement for those books, although you might not need them when using this one!

This book looks at a very few options in PowerPoint that can make a huge difference. It's like that famous 20:80 concept: 20 percent of the options can make 80 percent of the difference. So we'll fully cover that 20 percent to help you create better presentations in very little time.

How to Use This Book

A large number of pages cover the eight makeover chapters that are the raison d'être of this book. All these makeover chapters were written as do-it-yourself tutorials that are entirely self-contained. Peppered with visuals, each makeover can be finished at one sitting or whenever you have the time.

Each makeover is divided into individual steps, and you don't even have to start at the first step because we include a copy of the makeover presentation at the end of each step; you'll find it on the CD. Just choose which step you want to start with and get started. Thus, whether you have five minutes or five hours, there's something for everyone.

We also kept the makeovers independent of other programs, so we won't ask you to open Photoshop or some other program that you don't have and do something with it. Everything you learn to do within the covers of this book is possible using PowerPoint 2007.

How This Book Is Organized

This book is divided into three parts.

Part I: The Basics

Part I looks at how PowerPoint 2007 differs from earlier versions and gives a quick walkthrough of the interface and its elements.

Part II: The Makeovers

Part II is the heart of the book.

Chapter 2, "Makeover 1: A Corporate Presentation," is a typical corporate presentation that explains a new policy. Replacing clip art with photographs gives it a more sophisticated look.

Chapter 3, "Makeover 2: Medical Speaker Training," has lots of information on using charts and improving them with graphics and color.

Chapter 4 "Makeover 3: School Project," uses a "kid-friendly" look and shows you how a very simple presentation can be made to look elegant in little time.

Chapter 5, "Makeover 4: A Quick Team Presentation," explains how you can take slides from disparate sources and create a cohesive look with these seemingly different slides.

Chapter 6, "Makeover 5: Halloween Scrapbook," is a picture scrapbook presentation that gets "spooked out" with scary graphics and is set to eerie music.

Chapter 7, "Makeover 6: Kiosk Presentation," is in a kiosk in the entryway of the local high school. It lets the user view a map of the school, see a calendar of upcoming events, and get information about those events. This one gets jazzed up with some improvements to graphics and the addition of animation to the calendar.

Chapter 8, "Makeover 7: No Bullets Presentation," is an advertising tale: plenty of visuals and just the right amount of text. It's based on an award-winning presentation from Ethos3 Communications that takes a boring bulleted presentation to visual heaven.

Chapter 9, "Makeover 8: Trade Show Loop Presentation," uses high-impact animation to grab the viewers' attention. It's based on a makeover by Julie Terberg, the technical editor for this book.

Part III: Resources

Part III includes additional resources.

Chapter 10, "The Gallery," shows sample design layouts and inspiration.

Chapter 11, "Everything Else We Wanted to Squeeze In!": The title says it all! You will find this on the CD or at www.informit.com/title/9780789736819.

"On the CD," has specific information about what you'll find on the accompanying CD.

Who Should Use This Book?

Almost anyone with a basic understanding of Microsoft Windows and Office can use this book. We won't show you how you can open and save a file, but we will show you how to do everything else.

Beginners, intermediate users, and advanced users can benefit from this book and the concepts it introduces.

The Basics

I

Exploring PowerPoint 2007

At first glance, PowerPoint 2007 seems vastly different from PowerPoint 2003 and previous versions. It seems different because the interface, known as the Microsoft Office Fluent user interface, is unlike anything most of us have seen before. However, never fear— your favorite tools are still available. It won't be long before you speak fluent PowerPoint 2007 because it's really very easy to use!

Throughout the rest of this book, we explain every process step by step, and we also tell you which part of the interface you need to access. Even then, we cannot emphasize enough that reading this short chapter will be helpful, and 15 minutes is all it takes! Are you ready to get started?

The Interface

Throughout this book, we talk about the *Ribbon*, *tabs*, and *dialog launchers*, as well as other terms that might be unfamiliar to you. Understanding these terms is key to becoming fluent with the PowerPoint 2007 interface (see Figure 1.1), so take a look at the next few figures to see what's what.

After you've read this chapter (or even while you have this book open), launch PowerPoint 2007 and click all around the new stuff. It's all very intuitive and straightforward.

Quick Access Toolbar
Microsoft Office Button
Windows Control Menu

Ribbon

Slide
Pane

Task
Pane

Slide
Workspace

Status
Bar

Notes Pane

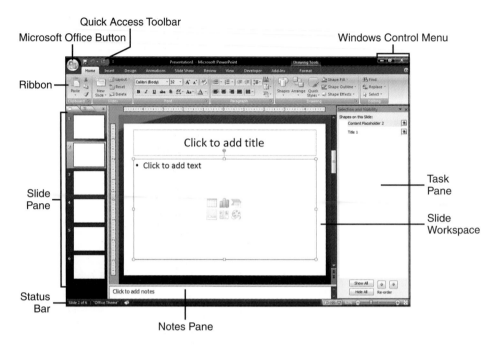

Figure 1.1

There are a number of different areas in the PowerPoint editing window when it is in Normal view.

Figure 1.1 shows you the new PowerPoint interface; here's an explanation of the interface elements:

- **Office Button**—The Office Button is where you work with your file. You'll find Save, Open, Print, and a variety of new tools, such as the Compatibility Checker and the Document Inspector, in this location. You also can access PowerPoint Options, where you can change various PowerPoint- and file-related settings, manage add-ins, and run diagnostics. If you have worked with PowerPoint before, you'll know this is an enhanced version of the old File menu.

- **Quick Access Toolbar (QAT)**—This is the one item you can customize in the Office interface. Click the small arrow next to it and choose More Commands to start the customization. You also can opt to show it below the Ribbon, where you'll have more room to add your favorite tools.

- **Windows Control menu**—The Minimize, Restore, and Close buttons are part of the Windows Control menu. They let you minimize and maximize the PowerPoint window. When you click the Close button, the current file closes. If you click the Close button when you have only one file open, PowerPoint itself will close.

The Ribbon

The Ribbon (see Figure 1.2) is the heart of the Office 2007 interface. It replaces the traditional menus and toolbars found in older versions of PowerPoint and other Office applications.

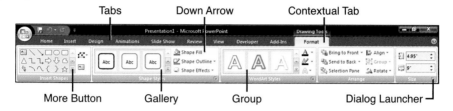

Figure 1.2

The area above the Ribbon that houses the Office Button, the Quick Access Toolbar, the filename, and the Windows Control menu buttons is not technically part of the Ribbon.

The Ribbon itself is a long, fixed-size strip that includes several interface elements of its own:

- **Tabs**—The Ribbon has several tabs; each tab is a collection of tools organized around a specific activity. For example, you will find animation and slide transition tools on the Animations tab. The most commonly used options are found on the Home tab. The Drawing Tools Format tab is the active tab shown in Figure 1.2.

- **Contextual tab**—Contextual tabs don't always show on the Ribbon; they appear only when you can use their tools on the object you've selected. For example, if you select a table, the Table Tools Design and Layout contextual tabs become available on the Ribbon. The Drawing Tools Format tab (seen in Figure 1.2) is a contextual tab; it is available because we've selected a text box in the workspace.

- **Group**—Chunks of related tools on a tab are known as groups. In Figure 1.2, you can see the Insert Shapes group, the Shape Styles group, the WordArt Styles group, the Arrange group, and the Size group.

- **Gallery**—Galleries are collections of thumbnails that represent a particular style or property. In Figure 1.2, you can see the Shape Styles gallery within the group of the same name. More often than not, these galleries can be expanded to form drop-down galleries by clicking the More button (see the next bullet). Whenever you hover your cursor over a gallery thumbnail, you can see how it will influence the selected slide object through the new *Live Preview* feature. Then just click any thumbnail in the gallery to apply that option.

- **More button**—Clicking the More button expands a gallery so that you can see all your options. Clicking the up and down arrows above a More button simply scrolls the choices in the gallery inside the Ribbon without expanding the gallery (see Figure 1.3).

Use these arrows to scroll through
gallery choices on the Ribbon
without expanding the gallery.   The More button expands galleries.

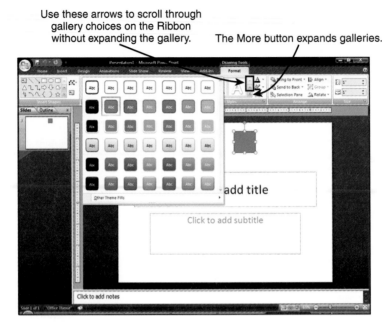

Figure 1.3

Click the More button to expand drop-down galleries.

- **Down arrow**—Click the downward-pointing arrow beside a tool on the Ribbon to display a gallery or additional options.
- **Dialog launcher**—The small square in the lower-right corner of some groups is a dialog launcher. It opens a related dialog box with more advanced options.

The Slide Pane

The Slide pane (see Figure 1.4) lets you move easily from slide to slide, select more than one slide at a time, delete slides, and rearrange them. You can switch between the Slide Thumbnails pane and the Outline View pane by clicking at the top of the Slide pane.

If you are looking for the Outlining toolbar found in previous PowerPoint versions, just right-click in the Outline View pane to find the same options.

The Slide Workspace

The Slide workspace (see Figure 1.5) is where you edit an individual slide. The slide you've selected in the Slides pane is the slide that shows up in the workspace.

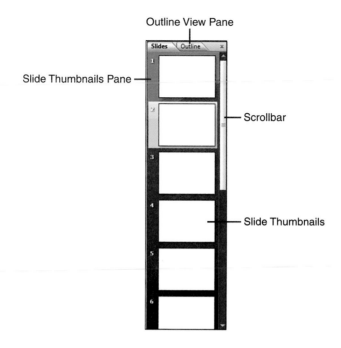

Figure 1.4

The yellow highlight in the Slides pane marks the selected slide, which is the slide that shows up in the workspace.

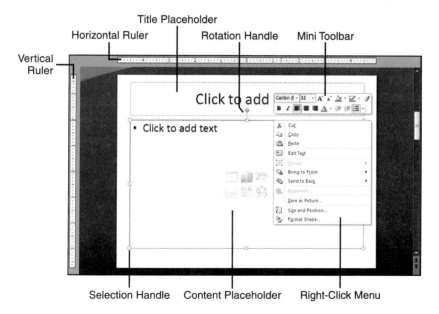

Figure 1.5

The Slide workspace is where you'll do the bulk of your work in PowerPoint.

At any point of time, your slide may or may not include these objects and interface elements:

- **Placeholders**—PowerPoint 2007 has a number of different kinds of placeholders: text, content, picture, and others. Placeholders are formatted and defined on Slide Masters and layouts. Using placeholders helps you maintain consistency throughout your presentation; you also can format them directly on the slides themselves if you prefer.

- **Mini toolbar**—The mini toolbar appears when you select text or right-click an object that can include text. It gives you quick access to the most popular formatting tools.

- **Right-click menu**—A contextual menu appears when you, well, right-click.

The Status Bar

The status bar (see Figure 1.6) shows information about your file. It also holds the zoom tools.

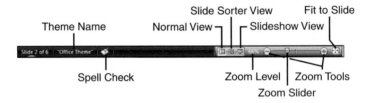

Figure 1.6
Zoom tools and information about the number of slides in the presentation can be found on the status bar.

Here's an explanation of some interface elements in the status bar:

- **Theme name**—The name of the theme that's been applied to the selected slide appears here.

- **View icons**—Click the appropriate view icon to switch to the Normal, Slide Sorter, or Slide Show view.

- **Zoom tools**—Click the Zoom level option to open a dialog box where you can specify your zoom level, or simply drag the caret on the Zoom slider.

- **Fit to Slide**—Click to return to full slide view after zooming.

New and Different Features

PowerPoint 2007 has a slew of great new features, and it also says good-bye to a few old friends.

New Features

There are many new features. Here are some of our favorites:

- **Office Themes**—Themes actually are Office-wide. They're similar to templates, but they allow you to maintain a common set of colors, fonts, and effects throughout your Word, PowerPoint, and Excel files.

- **Custom layouts, placeholders, and prompt text**—You now can create your own slide layouts! To go along with them, you now have the ability to add placeholders and change the "click here to add text" prompt to whatever you want.

- **SmartArt Graphics**—The new SmartArt Graphics option lets you create sleek diagrams with just a few clicks.

- **Text handling**—PowerPoint does a better job with basic text handling than ever before; for example, you now can kern text. In addition, underlines can be colored separately from text, tab settings apply to individual paragraphs of text instead of to the entire text box, and you have numeric control over tab placement.

- **Text effects**—The text engine was completely rewritten, and now text acts more like other drawing objects. Thus, in addition to better text handling in general, you now can apply slick effects—such as soft shadows, reflections, outlines, bevels, and picture fills—to regular, editable text.

- **Shape effects**—You know all that sweet stuff we said you can do with text? You can do them with drawing shapes, too. You even can make gradient lines now! In addition, you can convert shapes to freeforms, so that you can bend shapes to your will.

- **Picture effects**—In addition to new, theme-friendly recoloring tools, you also have one-click picture frames and edges. Very cool!

- **Quick Styles**—These are one-click, preset formatting options you can apply to almost any object.

- **Live preview**—Now you don't have to waste time applying formatting and then checking to see how it looks. Live preview does this on the fly when you run your mouse over selections in a gallery. Simply click the thumbnail in the gallery to accept and apply the formatting.

- **Nonmodal dialog boxes**—Some dialog boxes have the equivalent of live preview; that is, you don't have to specify a bunch of settings and then close the dialog box to see how it looks. With nonmodal dialog boxes, changes happen in real time, and you can select other objects on the slide without having to close the dialog box first.

- **Selection and Visibility pane**—This handy tool makes it easy to select objects on a slide, hide them, or change their stacking order. In addition, if you rename an object in this pane, the new name shows up in the Custom Animation pane, making your animation tasks much easier.

- **Editing within grouped objects**—You can resize and move individual objects within a group. Thus, you no longer have to ungroup items and lose their animation settings.

- **Ctrl+G and Ctrl+Alt+V**—We love that pressing Ctrl+G groups selected objects and pressing Ctrl+Alt+V opens the Paste Special dialog box.

- **Charting**—Charting now is done in Excel, giving PowerPoint users easy access to its powerful graphing features. In addition, chart parts work much like drawing objects, so all those shape and text effects can be applied to chart elements as well. Remember, you'll need to have Excel 2007 installed to access all the new charting options.

- **Chart templates**—You can save charts as chart templates and send them to other users. Unfortunately, chart templates don't travel with themes or templates, but at least it's a step in the right direction!

- **Tables**—Like so many other objects, tables got a facelift in PowerPoint 2007. Quick Styles make them look great right off the bat, and you finally can specify sizes for cell height and width.

- **Save as PDF**—Downloading and installing an add-in from http://office.microsoft.com lets you save files as PDFs. Be sure to save them as PowerPoint files first, or you won't be able to go back and edit them.

- **New file formats**—PowerPoint files now are XML-based. This doesn't mean a whole lot to the typical user, other than the file extensions now are four letters instead of three: PPTX, PPSX, and so on.

- **Slide libraries**—If you're lucky enough to have a Microsoft Office Sharepoint Server (MOSS) 2007 available, you have access to slide libraries, which allow you to upload and download slides, keep track of the latest version of a slide, and use the workflow services for your review process.

- **Mark as final**—This is a convenience marking, not a security feature. It tells users the file is considered to be the final one, and if they want to edit it, they must either click the Mark as Final button again to unmark it or save the file with a new name.

- **Compatibility Checker**—When you save your file in PPT/PPS format so that people using previous versions of PowerPoint can open it, the Compatibility Checker checks your file and tells you what will be uneditable.

- **Presenter view**—Presenter view got an overhaul, with bigger buttons, adjustable panes, and sizeable notes text.

Changed or Missing Features

This list is much, much shorter than the new features list:

- **Recolor Picture tool**—The Recolor Picture tool works differently than it used to, and the new tool doesn't let you recolor clip art or charts the way previous versions of PowerPoint did.

- **Insert Slides from File feature**—The Insert Slides from File feature now is located on the Home tab of the Ribbon. Click the bottom half of the New Slide button to open the New Slide gallery, and then choose Reuse Slides.

- **Macro recorder**—The macro recorder has been removed from PowerPoint 2007. The Microsoft Script Editor has been removed as well.

- **Customizing**—The Ribbon cannot be customized without third-party add-ins, and there are no more tear-away menus.

- **Select Multiple Objects tool**—The Select Multiple Objects tool doesn't exist in PowerPoint 2007, but who cares? You now have the Selection and Visibility pane, which is about a gazillion times better!

- **Insert From Scanner option**—This option was officially removed from Office 2007 applications, but you still can access it from the Clip Organizer.

- **Pattern fills and Lines**—If you rely on pattern fills and lines, you'll want to create your own pattern images and then apply them as a texture fill, because they no longer exist in PowerPoint 2007. However, all patterned fills and lines from previous versions of PowerPoint do show up in PowerPoint 2007 as long as you leave them unchanged.

- **Save as HTML option**—PowerPoint 2007 saves the same HTML as PowerPoint 2003 did. That means new features in PowerPoint 2007 won't display when you save the file as HTML.

- **Producer for PowerPoint**—Producer doesn't work with PowerPoint 2007.

- **Animation schemes**—Gone.

- **Send for Review option**—Zapped.

- **Presentation broadcasting**—Buh-bye.

The Makeovers

ISO 9001

Quality System Documentation
Requirements

Before

After

ON THE CD:

The sample presentation and all other files with which you need to work can be found on the CD in the `Makeover 01` folder.

2

Makeover 1: A Corporate Presentation

YOU WILL LEARN HOW TO:

■ Apply a Theme

■ Create a Slide Layout

■ Use Picture Placeholders

■ Rotate Pictures

■ Change Line Spacing

About This Makeover

Corporate presentations can be incredibly boring. Although we can't do a whole lot to help you with the subject matter of your presentations, we can at least help you make them look better!

To give this presentation some polish, we'll apply a PowerPoint 2007 theme, and we'll replace the clip art with photographs. Even these seemingly small changes can make a huge difference.

All photos in this presentation were graciously supplied by PhotoSpin.com.

Figure 2.1 shows you two slides from the "before" presentation; these are typical briefing slides seen in a million different offices throughout the world every day.

Figure 2.1
Basic, boring "before" slides.

You can see the same slides in Figure 2.2. It's really amazing how much difference a sophisticated theme and a few pictures can make!

Figure 2.2
Replacing clip art with photos has a huge impact.

Step 1.   Apply a Theme

Open the original presentation, `corporate_00.pptx`, by clicking Office Button, Open. This file can be found on the CD in the `Makeover 01\Steps` folder.

This presentation is a typical corporate presentation. It's dry, but someone added clip art in an attempt to jazz it up a bit. Applying an appropriate theme will immediately give it some class.

To apply a theme, follow these steps:

1. On the Design tab of the Ribbon, click the More button in the Themes gallery to view it as a drop-down gallery.

NOTE

When you move your mouse over thumbnails in a gallery, you can see how the respective formatting will look if you were to apply it to your content. This is called Live Preview. However, previewing doesn't actually *do* anything to your slides—you must click the thumbnail for that to happen.

---

2. Click the Module theme to apply it (see Figure 2.3). Module is a good template to use for corporate presentations. It's simple and sophisticated with a little drama on the title slides, but it's not opulent like, well, the Opulent theme is.

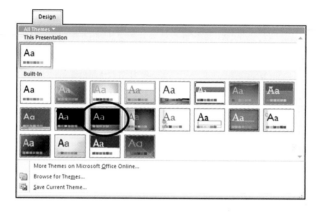

Figure 2.3

When you hover your mouse over a thumbnail in the Themes gallery, you can see how that formatting will look when it's applied to your content.

Step 2.   Create a Slide Layout

One of the best new features in PowerPoint 2007 is the ability to create your own layouts. We're going to take advantage of this by adding a new layout for text and pictures so that when we replace the clip art with photos, they'll be sized and cropped automatically.

If you are following the makeover step by step, continue using your saved presentation. If you just stepped in, you can use the `corporate_01.pptx` presentation from the Makeover 01\Steps folder on the CD.

Add the Layout

To create your own layout, follow these steps:

1. On the View tab of the Ribbon, click the Slide Master button to open Slide Master view.

2. On the Slide Master tab of the Ribbon, click Insert Layout to insert a new Slide Layout.

Add Placeholders to the Layout

Now that we've created a Slide Layout, we need to add some placeholders for text and pictures. Here's how to do it:

1. With the new, inserted layout active, click Insert Placeholder on the Ribbon to view the Placeholder gallery, and then click Text (see Figure 2.4).

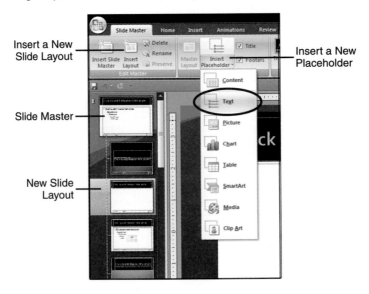

Figure 2.4

Use the Insert Placeholder gallery to add a placeholder to a Slide Layout.

2. Click and drag on the slide to create the text placeholder right below the slide title area, and toward the left part of the slide (refer to Figure 2.5). Resize if required.

3. Click Insert Placeholder on the Ribbon again, but this time, choose Picture from the Placeholder gallery.

4. Click and drag on the right part of the slide to create the picture placeholder (see Figure 2.5). Resize if required.

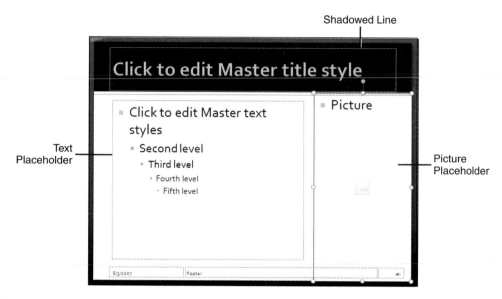

Figure 2.5

You can add more than one placeholder to a slide. This slide has a text placeholder and a picture placeholder.

It can be difficult to align the bottom of one object with the top of another. In this instance, it's difficult to align the top of the picture placeholder with the bottom of the shadowed line just beneath the black area that defines the title (see Figure 2.5).

If we were working on a slide instead of the Slide Masters and layouts, we'd just size the picture placeholder so that it's close enough, and then use the Arrange tools or the Selection Pane to bring the shadowed line above the picture placeholder. However, because the shadowed line is on the Slide Master, we can't change its position or layer on the actual slides; items on the Slide Master and layouts always appear beneath the objects on the slides themselves. Think of the masters and layouts as the bottom layer of the slide.

In this case, just zoom up close using the Zoom tool on the status bar, and you'll be able to see where the shadow on the line ends and the picture placeholder should begin. You also can click the Drawing Tools Format tab on the Ribbon, click the Size and Position dialog launcher, and on the Size tab, type **5.83** for the height and **3.08** for the width. On the Position tab, specify **6.92** for the horizontal position, and **1.67** for the vertical (see Figure 2.6). Click Close to get the dialog box out of the way.

Size and Position
Dialog Launcher

Figure 2.6
The Size and Position dialog box lets you place objects by the numbers.

Align the left edges of the text and title placeholders by doing the following:

1. Select the title placeholder and the text placeholder. The title placeholder should be farther to the left than the text placeholder (refer to Figure 2.5).

2. On the Drawing Tools Format tab of the Ribbon, click Align, and then click Align Left (see Figure 2.7). You also can access these tools from the Home tab of the Ribbon by clicking Arrange and then clicking Align.

3. Deselect both the title and text placeholders, and then select just the text placeholder. Drag the right edge of this placeholder so that it's close to the picture placeholder, but not right up against it. You want to keep a little breathing room between your picture and the text (refer to Figure 2.7).

Name the Layout

Finally, we'll give our custom Slide Layout a name by right-clicking the layout thumbnail in the Slides pane, choosing Rename Layout, and typing **Text and Picture** (see Figure 2.8).

Figure 2.7

The Alignment tools help you position objects on your slides relative to other objects or to the slide itself.

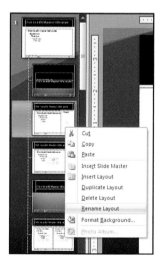

Figure 2.8

You can access a number of tools by right-clicking slide thumbnails in Slide Master view.

Click the Close Slide Master View button on the Slide Master tab of the Ribbon (or click Normal on the View tab of the Ribbon) to get back to Normal editing view.

Step 3.   Apply the Slide Layout to Existing Slides

To make the new layout available on our slides (complete with picture and text placeholders), we must apply it to the slides.

If you are following the makeover step by step, continue using your saved presentation. If you just stepped in, you can use the **corporate_02.pptx** presentation from the Makeover 01\Steps folder on the CD.

To apply a layout to a slide, follow these steps:

1. Click slide 2 in the Slides pane.

2. Press and hold the Shift button, and then scroll down and click slide 7 in the Slides pane. This selects slides 2–7.

3. On the Home tab of the Ribbon, click Layout.

4. From the Layout gallery, choose the layout we created (it is named Text and Picture). When you click it, it will be applied to the slides we selected (see Figure 2.9).

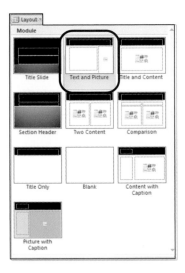

Figure 2.9
Slide layouts are your friends; they help keep objects and placement consistent from slide to slide.

Step 4.   Add Pictures to the Picture Placeholder

We'll replace the clip art in this presentation with photographs. Photos are much more sophisticated than most clip art, and you easily can find appropriate photos for a reasonable cost.

TIP

If you do many presentations, you might want to look into purchasing some royalty-free stock photo CDs or a download subscription so that you'll have what you need at your fingertips. Check http://www.pptkit.com/media for links to several stock media sites.

There are many ways to add pictures to your presentations. In this chapter, we've used the picture placeholder because it automatically crops pictures to fill the placeholder, and that often makes the pictures look way cool. (You'll learn other methods of inserting pictures in some of the other makeovers.)

If you are following the makeover step by step, continue using your saved presentation. If you just stepped in, you can use the **corporate_03.pptx** presentation from the Makeover 0\Steps1 folder on the CD.

1. Click slide 2 in the Slides pane.

2. Delete the clip art from the slide.

3. Click the icon in the picture placeholder (see Figure 2.10) to open the Insert Picture dialog box.

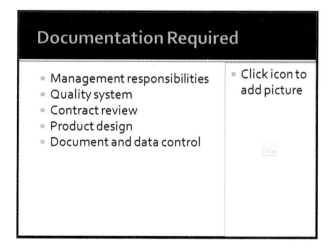

Figure 2.10

As the text says, click the icon in the placeholder to add a picture.

4. Select an appropriate picture and click Insert. We used picture 14_2503379 from PhotoSpin, and it's included on the Makeover 01\Pictures folder on the CD.

TIP

Picture placeholders are different from content placeholders. Both allow you to click an icon to add something to your slide, but a picture placeholder crops your picture automatically to fill the placeholder. A content placeholder just sizes the picture proportionately within the area specified by the placeholder.

5. Repeat steps 1–4 for the rest of the slides, using the PhotoSpin-supplied images in the Makeover 01\Pictures folder on the CD. We used 10_2502557 for slide 3, 2120008 for slide 4, 10_2502337 for slide 5, 2160249 for slide 6, and 1080012 for slide 7.

CONSIDER CLIP ART STYLES

Clip art is a broad term that often includes drawings and photos. More often than not though, clip art means drawings and illustrations that are available by the bucket load in collections that can include millions of individual clip art pieces. Naturally, you can't expect entire collections to sport the same *style*.

So what do we mean by style? That's a broad term that indicates how the designs are tailored. For example, a group of clip art might use thick black lines and bold colors. Another group might use a monochromatic blue palette, and yet another piece might not include any style at all that's consistent with others in the collection.

If you're using clip art, at least use something that's the same style. Using clip art that is completely dissimilar can detract from a presentation and make your presentation shout "amateur at work."

For example, if you look at the clip art at Office Online (go to http://office.microsoft.com, and then click the tab for clip art) and click the magnifying glass to look at more information on a clip, you'll see Style listed as one of the parameters (see Figure 2.11). Click that style, and you can see all the other clips in that same style (see Figure 2.12). Choose from one style of clip, and you won't go wrong.

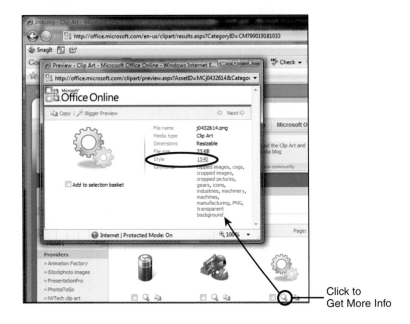

Figure 2.11

Clicking the magnifying glass gives you more information about a clip on Office Online. From there, you can find out the style of the clip.

Figure 2.12

Office Online search results for one style of clip art.

A general rule of thumb is that you want people (and sometimes things) to be facing into your slide, not looking off the page. The picture of the forklift (which we added to slide 4) is a good example. It should be facing the opposite direction, moving onto the slide instead of off it (see Figure 2.13). That's easy enough to fix by following these steps:

1. Select the picture on the slide.

Figure 2.13

The forklift picture faces the wrong way.

2. On the Home tab of the Ribbon, choose Arrange, Rotate, and then Flip Horizontal (see Figure 2.14).

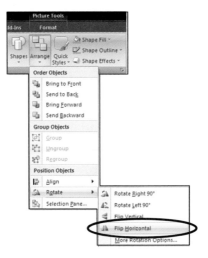

Figure 2.14

Use the Rotate and Flip tools to make pictures face the opposite direction and to turn a shot from horizontal to vertical, or vice versa.

Now that we've finished adding and manipulating the pictures, all that's left is to finish the text.

Step 5.   Fine-tune Your Text

After you've gotten the basics of your presentation together, you might find that you need to tweak some things. For example, on slides 3 and 4, you can see that when the text drops to a second line, all the bullets run together (refer to Figure 2.13). We will tweak the line spacing to help the reader distinguish one point from another.

If you are following the makeover step by step, continue using your saved presentation. If you just stepped in, you can use the `corporate_04.pptx` presentation from the Makeover 01\Steps folder on the CD.

Change Line Spacing on the Slide Layout

Here's how to fix line spacing:

1. On the View tab of the Ribbon, click Slide Master to open Slide Master view.

2. Click the Text and Picture layout in the Slides pane.

3. Click the top level of text in the placeholder in the spot where it says "Click to Edit Master Text Styles."

TIP

If you want to apply the same line spacing settings to all levels of text, select the placeholder. When the placeholder is selected, the selection border appears as a solid line.

If you want to apply different settings to each level, just click that level of text inside the place-holder. The selection border will show as a dotted line to indicate that your changes affect individual lines rather than the entire placeholder (see Figure 2.15).

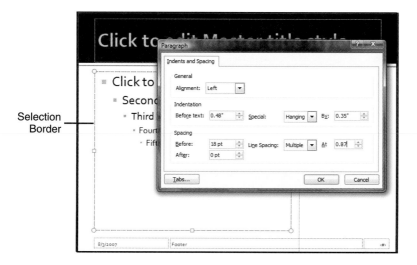

Figure 2.15

Tweak line spacing settings in the Paragraph dialog box, which can be launched by clicking its dialog launcher on the Home tab of the Ribbon.

4. On the Home tab of the Ribbon, click the Paragraph dialog launcher.

5. In the Paragraph dialog box, specify Line Spacing as Multiple at **.87** and Spacing Before at **18** pt (see Figure 2.15). Click OK to apply the settings and close the dialog box.

TIP

Don't specify both Before and After line spacing settings. Choose one or the other and use it. Setting both Before and After spacing options makes it more difficult to edit long lists of text.

6. On the Slide Master tab of the Ribbon, click Close Master View to return to Normal editing view. You'll be able to spot the changes in line spacing on Slide 3 right away.

Turn Off Autofitting and Reapply Line Spacing to One Slide

PowerPoint's text autofitting is not as heavy-handed as it was in the past, but the results still might not be satisfactory. In this presentation, it's squishing the text on slide 4 a little. To correct it, follow these steps:

1. Right-click the text placeholder on slide 4 and choose Format Shape.

2. In the Text Box area, choose Do not Autofit (see Figure 2.16). Click Close to close the dialog box.

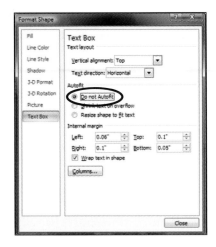

Figure 2.16

Access more advanced settings in the Format Shape dialog box. Right-click almost any object to open this dialog box.

3. Change the font size by typing **30** into the Font Size box on the Home tab of the Ribbon and pressing Enter (see Figure 2.17).

Figure 2.17

Basic font attributes such as size, font face, and color are available on the Home tab of the Ribbon.

TIP

Some people don't like to leave one word hanging alone on the last line of a bullet. It's a left-over from desktop publishing standards, where those dangling words are known as *widows and orphans*.

PowerPoint 2007 has text kerning capabilities (click the Font dialog launcher on the Home tab to use them). These capabilities enable you to adjust the spacing between characters within a word, but they won't always be enough to do the trick. If you need to force a line break to move text to the next line, place your cursor where you want the line break and press Shift+Enter. This creates what is known as a *soft return*; it creates a new line, but not a new paragraph with a new bullet point (see Figure 2.18).

Figure 2.18
Press Shift+Enter to add soft returns and remove widows and orphans where appropriate.

See? Just a few simple changes can take your presentation from "ow" to "wow!" If you have been fol-lowing the makeover step by step, take a minute to review your saved presentation. If you want to see what the final made-over presentation looks like, you can open the `corporate_05.pptx` presentation from the `Makeover 01\Steps` folder on the CD.

Sukomu Speaker Training

Tom Thumb, MD
President, Nailbiters Anonymous
Director of Education, Beautiful Hands America

Before

After

3

Makeover 2: Medical Speaker Training

About This Makeover

Many presenters find it disconcerting to see their presentations completely changed—they don't recognize them and become extremely stressed as a result. Thus, rather than completely overhauling this presentation, our goal is to create consistency throughout the slides and make them visually interesting, yet easy to read and understand quickly. Sukomu, Inc., will use this presentation for a medical speaker training meeting to teach healthcare professionals about their new drug, Chewaway.

One simple thing you can do to help a presentation look more professional and pulled together is to use placeholders to make sure that various text elements—titles, references, and so on—are positioned in the same location on all slides throughout the file. PowerPoint 2007 allows the user to do this by creating her own placeholders, so take advantage of this new feature.

Figure 3.1 shows you two slides from the "before" presentation; these are conventional slides that look similar to the millions of slides churned out in offices every single day.

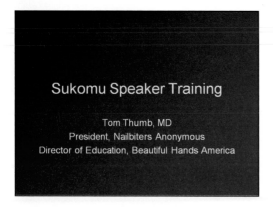
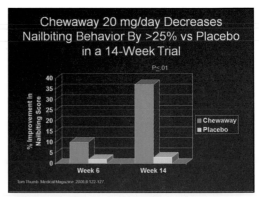

Figure 3.1

You've seen these types of slides everywhere.

Figure 3.2 shows you the same slides, but as you can see, these have more pizzazz in them even though they really aren't too different from the slides in Figure 3.1.

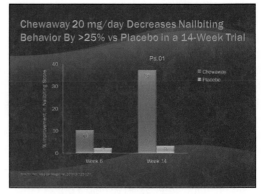

Figure 3.2

Some smart housekeeping with themes and layouts can create a makeover.

To create consistency in the slides, we will apply a theme, adjust the title placeholders, and put reference text into placeholders on some of the Slide Layouts.

Step 1.   Apply a Theme

A *theme* consists of a color scheme, a font set, effects, Slide Masters, Slide Layouts, and background styles. Applying a theme to your presentation is the best way to ensure that these elements remain consistent throughout the file.

TIP

Remember, these same themes can also be used in Word 2007 and Excel 2007.

Follow these steps to get started:

1. Open the original presentation, `medical_00.pptx`, by clicking Office Button, Open.

2. Now you need to apply a medical theme that we included on the CD. Click the Design tab on the Ribbon. Click the More arrow to the far right of the Themes gallery (see Figure 3.3) to display all the available theme choices.

Figure 3.3

Click the More arrow on the Ribbon to display the full gallery with all the choices.

3. Click Browse for Themes (see Figure 3.4).

Figure 3.4

See how different themes will look when applied to your slide by mousing over any of the thumbnails in the Themes gallery.

4. Navigate to the `medical.thmx` file in the `Makeover 02\Theme` folder on the CD, and click Apply.

NOTE

To apply a theme to only a few slides, select them in the Slides pane (or Slide Sorter view), right-click any of the thumbnails in the Themes gallery, and choose Apply to Selected Slides.

WORKING WITH SLIDE MASTERS AND LAYOUTS

If you want something to appear on every slide, you should place it on the *Slide Master*.

If you want something to appear on a specific type of slide, you should place it on the Slide Layout(s). For example, if you want your corporate logo to appear only on your title slides, add the logo to the Title Slide Layout, not to the Slide Master. In addition, if you want a different font face on the title slide, change that on the Title Slide Layout, not on the Slide Master.

To work with Slide Masters and Layouts, click the View tab, and click Slide Master to open Slide Master view.

A Slide Master is the design basis for each of your individual slides. Each Slide Master also has related Slide Layouts that control how individual slides look.

The large thumbnail in the Slides pane is the Slide Master. The smaller thumbnails below the large thumbnail are Slide Layouts. The design of the Slide Layout is based on the Slide Master above it in the Slides pane (see Figure 3.5). You can have more than one Slide Master in a presentation.

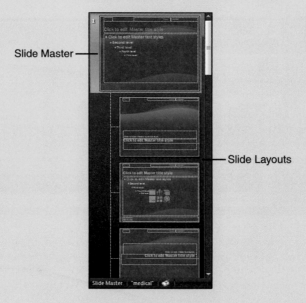

Slide Master —

— Slide Layouts

Figure 3.5
Slide Layouts inherit settings from the Slide Master.

Consider carefully whether to include another Slide Master with its collateral layouts or simply add a Slide Layout to an existing master (see Figure 3.6). This is not always an easy decision to make. You might need to have one master for every layout that includes a logo and a second master for every layout that is without a logo. On the other hand, you might prefer to include just a few individual layouts with a logo and a few without, all attached to the same Slide Master.

Whichever way you go, delete extra Slide Layouts you are sure you won't need, as they do add to file size (and also make it confusing for you to choose from a crowded layout gallery).

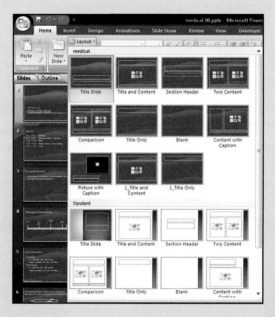

Figure 3.6

When you click the Home tab on the Ribbon and then click New Slide to add a slide to your presentation, all Slide Masters and their collateral layouts are displayed for you. As you can see, this gallery can become crowded quickly!

When you are done, you can exit the Slide Master view by selecting the Slide Master tab, and then clicking the Close Master View button. Alternatively, click Normal on the View tab.

Step 2.   Anchor the Text in the Title Placeholder

Slide titles rarely are the same length; they vary from one line of text to two lines of text and often include more lines still. When you add title text, usually the title placeholder expands on both the top and the bottom to make room for the text. This causes the baseline of the title text to jump and "descend" as you move from one slide to another during a presentation.

To avoid this type of distracting design (see slide 6 in the original presentation for an example), anchor the baseline of the text at the bottom of the placeholder.

TIP

Repeating elements, such as slide titles and references, that don't jump around as you move from slide to slide indicate a professionally developed presentation.

If you are following the makeover step by step, continue using your saved presentation. If you just stepped in, you can use the `medical_02.pptx` presentation from the `Makeover 02\Steps` folder on the CD.

To anchor the text in the title placeholder, do the following:

1. Click the View tab on the Ribbon, and choose Slide Master to open Slide Master view.

2. Select the Slide Master by clicking the larger thumbnail on the top in the Slides pane. You might have to scroll up to the top of the Slides pane if the Slide Master is not visible, and then select the title placeholder in the Slide Master.

3. Right-click the title placeholder, and choose Format Shape to open the Format Shape dialog box (see Figure 3.7).

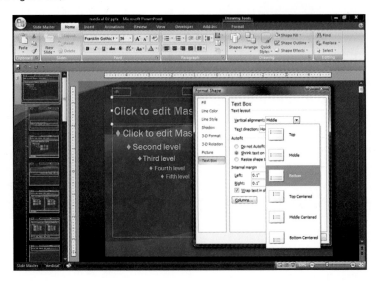

Figure 3.7

Anchor your text in the Format Shape dialog box.

4. In the Format Shape dialog box, click Text Box on the left and choose Bottom from the Vertical Alignment drop-down list on the right (refer again to Figure 3.7).

5. Click Close to close the dialog box and get it out of your way.

6. Click the View tab on the Ribbon, and then choose Normal to return to Normal editing view. You also can click the Slide Master tab on the Ribbon and choose Close Master View.

TIP

By default, any change applied to the Slide Master also reflects on all the Slide Layouts based on it. At the Slide Layout level, you can override these changes as required.

FITTING AND PLACING TITLES

Be sure to allow room for at least two-line titles when creating your Slide Masters and layouts.

Use title placeholders—that's what they're there for! Placeholders help ensure that your text is in the same place every time so that the titles don't appear to jump around on the screen as you move from slide to slide.

If a title is longer than two lines, decrease the font size of the text on the actual slide so that it fits on two lines.

Use the Character Spacing option (click the Home tab on the Ribbon, Font dialog launcher, Character Spacing) to condense the text slightly to squeeze a title into two lines. Don't overdo it!

If a title absolutely won't fit on two lines without looking extremely out of place, then by all means, keep it on three lines. Sometimes you have to do what you have to do. If there are obvious edits you can make that will help fit the title onto two lines, consider suggesting them to the presenter.

Step 3.   Putting the Placeholders to Work

To ensure that the theme formatting is applied, we must reset the Slide Layout for the title slide. We also need to apply the correct layout to the rest of our slides. Sometimes PowerPoint gets mixed up and applies the wrong Slide Layouts when you apply a theme. This is one of those times, but it's easy to correct. If you don't understand all this stuff, don't worry; just follow this quick series of steps that will teach you exactly what you need to learn.

If you are following the makeover step by step, continue using your saved presentation. If you just stepped in, you can use the `medical_03.pptx` presentation from the Makeover 02\Steps folder on the CD.

Reset the Slide Layout

Follow these steps to reset the Slide Layout:

1. Select the Title Slide in the Slides pane.

2. On the Home tab on the Ribbon, choose Reset in the Slides group.

The result is nicely formatted text that is readable and visually appealing (see Figure 3.8).

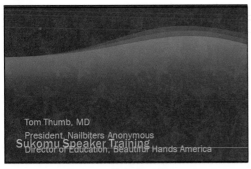
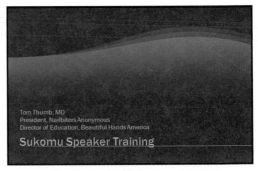

Before   After

Figure 3.8

Resetting the Slide Layout strips any manual formatting and applies the position, size, and formatting of the slide placeholders.

Apply Appropriate Layouts as Necessary

We created some layouts with a reference placeholder so that our references could be in the same position from slide to slide. We need to apply these layouts to the slides.

To apply a different Slide Layout

1. Select slides 2, 3, 5, and 7 in the Slides pane (or in Slide Sorter view) by Ctrl+clicking on each thumbnail.

2. On the Home tab on the Ribbon, choose Layout, and then the Title and Content layout (see Figure 3.9).

3. Similarly, apply the Title Only Slide Layout to slides 4 and 6.

4. Finally, select slides 2 through 7 and on the Home tab of the Ribbon, choose Reset to apply the placeholder formatting to the selected slides. Now see? I told you it was easy!

Add Text to Placeholders

The next thing you need to do with the existing medical presentation is to paste the reference text into the reference placeholders so that they'll be properly positioned.

Select the reference text on slide 5, copy it, and paste it into the reference placeholder (where it says Add Reference Here). Then delete the old reference text box if necessary. Repeat this process for the references on slide 6, and save your file.

NOTE

The default paste behavior will be to use destination theme, which means the pasted text will pick up the formatting you've already specified in the placeholder. That is why it makes sense to format the placeholder before you put text into it.

Figure 3.9

The Slide Layout gallery displays the Slide Layouts included in your presentation. Simply click one to choose the layout of your slide.

NOTE

Empty placeholders don't display in Slide Show view, so don't worry about them containing no text; you can leave them as they are.

Step 4.   Add and Format Tabs for Uniform Alignment

Sometimes you don't need a full-fledged table, but your text could still benefit from alignment that is better than what a couple taps of the spacebar can provide. In those situations, PowerPoint's tabs sure come in handy!

If you are following the makeover step by step, just continue using your saved presentation. If you just stepped in, you can use the **medical_03.pptx** presentation from the Makeover 02\Steps folder on the CD.

We added tabs on slide 2 to better align the times on the agenda and to make them easier to read at a glance—it's much better than trying to eyeball it using the spacebar!

To add tabs on a slide, do the following:

1. Right-click the edge of the text placeholder on slide 2 so that you don't select any individual text. On the mini toolbar that shows up, click the bullet icon to remove the bullets from the text.

2. Click before the first time (8:00) and press Tab.

3. Between 8:00 and the dash, delete the space and press Tab again.

4. Between the dash and 9:00, delete the space and press Tab again.

5. Between 9:00 and the word Breakfast, delete the space and press Tab once more. Repeat steps 2–5 for the rest of the lines. For now, don't worry if the text spills over to the next line or if it looks as if the tab is not there (see Figure 3.10).

Now position the tab stops. The first is a right-aligned tab to align the right edges of the first numbers.

1. If the ruler isn't visible, turn it on by clicking the View tab on the Ribbon and placing a check in the Ruler check box.

2. Select all the text.

CAUTION

Unlike in PowerPoint 2003 and earlier, PowerPoint 2007 tabs apply to only one paragraph of text, not to the entire text box, so you must select the text to which you want to apply the tab.

---

3. Slide the bottom indent caret (refer to Figure 3.10) on the ruler all the way to the left to remove the indent from the text. Don't panic if the text shifts to the right, because you'll fix this in the next steps.

Figure 3.10
Tabs have been added to this slide, but they have not been positioned.

4. Note that the tab selector on the far left shows the left align tab by default. Clicking it in succession rotates between center, right, and justified align tabs. Click it twice so that the right-aligned tab is showing (see Figure 3.11).

5. Click the bottom edge of the ruler to add a tab. You don't need to worry about how far along the ruler you click because you'll reposition the tab next.

6. Click and drag the new tab stop marker on the ruler to a position where you want the right-most characters in the opening set of timings to anchor (use Figure 3.11 as a reference).

TIP

Press the Ctrl key while dragging the tab marker on the ruler for finer control.

7. With all the text still selected, repeat steps 4–6 using a center tab for the dash, another right tab for the ending time, and a left-aligned tab for the session description (see Figure 3.12).

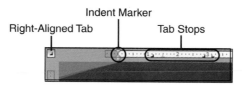

Figure 3.11

You can see the tab selector on the left and the tab stops indicated on the ruler.

TIP

You also can use the Tab dialog box, a new feature in PowerPoint 2007. Click the Home tab on the Ribbon, the Paragraph dialog launcher, and then the Tabs button.

8. Capitalize the words Training Skills and Workshop. Alternatively, make the words Product and Information lowercased. It doesn't really matter which you do, just be consistent.

9. Finally, select the Chewaway Product Information line of text, right-click it, and then select Light Yellow, Accent 3 from the Font Color drop-down list on the mini toolbar. Repeat this step for the Speaker Training Skills Workshop text. This helps the reader's eye distinguish the topic from the others as she reads down the list. See Figure 3.12 to see how the finished slide looks.

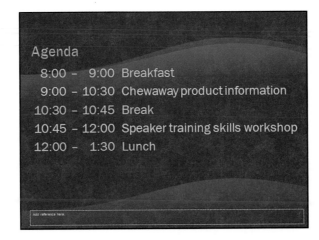

Figure 3.12
The new agenda slide is much easier to read. All it took was a few tabs!

Step 5.   Use SmartArt Diagrams

SmartArt diagrams are a new feature in PowerPoint 2007. They make it easy for you to create organization charts, flow charts, process plans, and other types of diagrams and to apply formatting that coordinates well with your presentation. Why not save yourself some hassle and use SmartArt instead of drawing diagrams from scratch?

SmartArt diagrams are just what you need for the timeline graphic in this makeover. Here we inserted the Closed Chevron Process diagram and chose 3D Inset from the SmartArt Styles gallery.

If you are following the makeover step by step, continue using your saved presentation. If you just stepped in, you can use the **medical_04.pptx** presentation from the Makeover 02\Steps folder on the CD.

Add and Format a SmartArt Diagram

Insert a SmartArt diagram following these steps:

1. On slide 4, click the Insert tab on the Ribbon, and then click SmartArt. This brings up the Choose a SmartArt Graphic dialog box.

2. Choose the Process category on the left pane of the dialog box, and select Closed Chevron Process from the list in the middle of the dialog box (see Figure 3.13).

3. Click OK to close the dialog box and add the diagram to your slide.

4. Click the double-headed arrow on the left of the SmartArt diagram to open the SmartArt Text pane (if it is not already visible). Type the months January through June in this pane (see Figure 3.14).

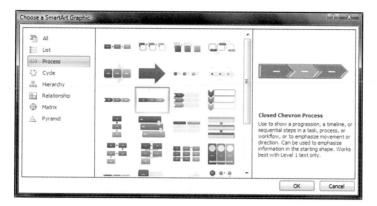

Figure 3.13

You can choose from a wide variety of SmartArt diagram types.

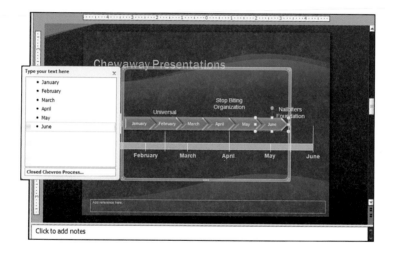

Figure 3.14

The Text Pane in a SmartArt graphic lets you add new shapes by typing a new bullet.

5. On the SmartArt Tools Design tab of the Ribbon, choose SmartArt Styles gallery. Click the More drop-down arrow to view the entire gallery. Click the 3D Inset style (see Figure 3.15) to apply it.

TIP

To change a shape in the diagram, select a shape and choose SmartArt Tools Format, Change Shape. Choose a different shape from the Shapes gallery.

---

6. Drag the edges of the diagram to resize the entire diagram and place it on the middle of the slide, generally in the same position as the existing timeline. You might want to click the close button on the Text pane before you do the resizing.

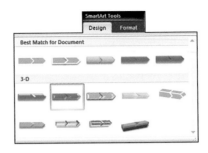

Figure 3.15

The SmartArt styles gallery gives you a number of 2D and 3D effects to make your SmartArt stylish with just one click. By mousing over a style in the gallery, you can see what it would look like applied to your diagram.

TIP

You can also click the SmartArt Tools Format tab and choose Size if you need to work with more exact measurements.

---

7. With the SmartArt graphic selected, click the Home tab on the Ribbon, and then click Arrange, Send to Back.

8. On the slide itself, delete the January through June text boxes, the lines pointing to February, March, May, and June, and the rectangle that represents the timeline (see Figure 3.16).

Format the Events Labels and Lines

Although the basis of most timelines can be added with the SmartArt tool, often you need to add other lines and shapes to complete the diagram. We've use PowerPoint's shapes and lines to add labels for individual events on the timeline.

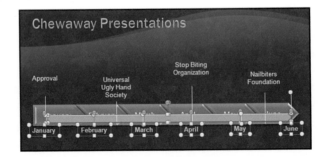

Figure 3.16

Send the SmartArt diagram behind other objects on the slide so that you can easily select and delete them.

Give the lines pointing to the events a little depth so that they don't look so flat against the 3D timeline:

1. Select each of the lines by Shift+clicking each line.

2. Click the Home tab on the Ribbon, and choose Shape Outline, Weight, 2 1/4 pt.

3. With the lines still selected, choose Shape Effects, Bevel, Cool Slant (see Figure 3.17).

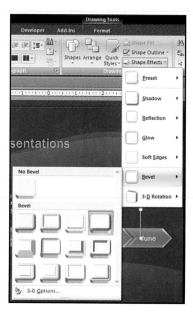

Figure 3.17

Shape fills, outlines, and effects are available on the Home tab and the Drawing Tools Format tab of the Ribbon.

Aligning the tops of the event label text boxes does not look good because it creates a very large gap between some of the lines and the event labels (see Figure 3.18). One workaround to that is to vary the length of the lines. Another is to align the horizontal middle of the text boxes. We chose to widen the Universal Ugly Hand Society text box so that it spans two lines instead of three. This helps make the labels more consistent, because all the other labels are one or two lines.

1. Shift+click to select the event text boxes.

2. Click the Home tab on the Ribbon, and then click Arrange, Align, Align Bottom.

NOTE

To create the soft return line break, place the cursor between the words Universal and Ugly and press Shift+Enter. Attention to these details will go a long way toward making your presentation look more polished.

---

3. Shift+click to select the event lines.

4. Click the Home tab on the Ribbon, and then choose Arrange, Align, Align Top.

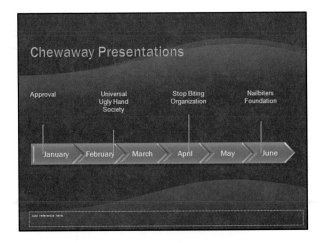

Figure 3.18

Don't be afraid to experiment with the alignment of objects on the slide. As you can see here, aligning the tops of the event label text boxes doesn't work very well because of the inconsistent gaps between the text and the vertical lines.

5. Finally, select the SmartArt diagram, click the Home tab on the Ribbon, and then choose Arrange, Bring to Front to reposition the diagram on the layer on top of the lines that point to each event. This makes the lines look as if they were extending from the timeline (see Figure 3.19).

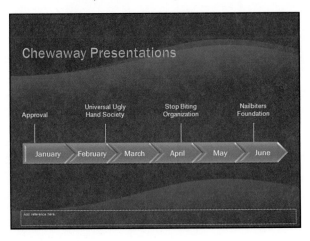

Figure 3.19

Align the bottoms of the event labels and the tops of the lines pointing to them. Attention to these types of details will make your presentation look more polished.

NOTE

If the Bring to Front option is not available in the Arrange drop-down list, you have probably selected an object inside the SmartArt diagram instead of the diagram itself. (Sometimes it's hard to tell!) To make the function available, click the edge of the SmartArt diagram and try again.

If you have more event labels than our makeover presentation has, no problem! Extend some lines and place labels below the timeline. Add more labels above the first row. Abbreviate text. Highlight the more important dates. Be creative. However, do try your best to make the timeline clean and concise and the labels and lines well-aligned. See Figures 3.20 and 3.21 for a few examples.

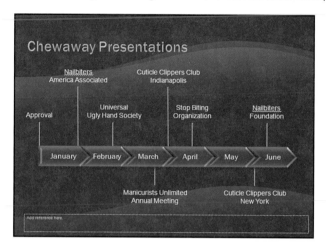

Figure 3.20

One way to make room for multiple labels is to stagger the lengths of the leader lines. Notice that each text box is aligned with other text boxes in the same row and is centered with its leader line.

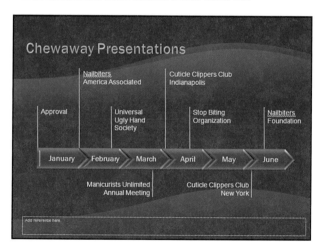

Figure 3.21

Here is another example of a timeline with multiple rows of labels. Notice that each text label is aligned both with the line pointing to it and with other labels in the row.

Step 6.   Create a Table

One way to display information and make it easier to grasp quickly is to use a table. PowerPoint 2007 tables are easy to use and format, so be sure to take advantage of this feature.

If you are following the makeover step by step, continue using your saved presentation. If you just stepped in, you can use the **medical_05.pptx** presentation from the Makeover 02\Steps folder on the CD.

Slide 5 (see Figure 3.22) could benefit from a better display to make the data easier to read. We used a table because they make information easier to grasp (and they look so good in PowerPoint 2007!).

Here's how to work with a table:

1. Click the Insert tab on the Ribbon, and then select Table. Drag to select the number of columns and rows you want. We used 3×3, as you can see in Figure 3.23

2. Type the content for the table (see Figure 3.24).

3. On the Table Tools Design tab on the Ribbon, click the More arrow at the far right of the Table Styles gallery so that you can see the various options. We used the Table quick style Medium Style 2 – Accent 1.

4. Click the edge of the table to select it. Click the Table Tools Layout tab on the Ribbon, and then select Alignment, Center Vertically to vertically align all text in the center of its row.

5. Select the cells in the Chewaway and Placebo columns by clicking and dragging your mouse in them. Click the Table Tools Layout tab of the Ribbon, and then select Alignment, Center Horizontally to center the text in the cells.

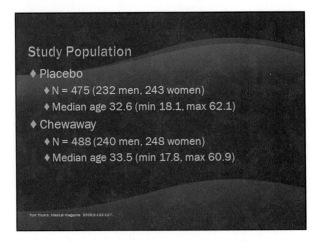

Figure 3.22

This mess of data could benefit from the structure of a table.

Figure 3.23

Click and drag to specify the number of columns and rows you want your table to have.

6. Double-click the vertical edge between the first and second column to automatically resize the first column.

7. Drag the bottom edge of the table to make it taller.

8. Press Shift+Enter in each cell to move the male/female and minimum/maximum information to the next line. Make the font size for this text smaller if you wish. This helps highlight the most important information.

9. Click the Home tab on the Ribbon, and then click Layout, Title Only to change the Slide Layout. Delete the text box with the original text.

Figure 3.24 shows how the finished table looks with all the formatting changes applied.

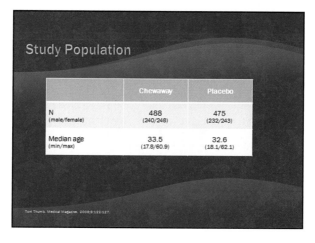

Figure 3.24

A table is a good choice for displaying this type of information.

TIP

Don't forget to use the vertical alignment options on the Table Tools Layout tab in the Alignment group. Even just setting all cells to center vertically will make your table look more polished.

Tables are pretty easy to navigate and format. The following guidelines can be used sequentially, or you could just use the ones that are relevant for a particular table:

- Click in a table cell, and drag your mouse to select text in entire columns, rows, or cells.
- Use the up- and down-arrow keys to move vertically or the right- and left-arrow keys to move horizontally, or you can just click in a cell with your mouse.
- Use the Tab key to move from cell to cell. Pressing the Tab key in the last cell of a table adds a new row automatically. Shift+Tab moves you backward through the cells.
- Use Ctrl+Tab to add a tab stop in a cell. Adjust it by dragging the tab marker on the Ruler. (If necessary, turn on your ruler by selecting the View tab, then Ruler.)
- Choose the Table Tools Layout tab, and then select Alignment, Align Top, Center Vertically, or Align Bottom to control the vertical placement of text in a cell. You also can use the left-align, center, and right-align tools to control the horizontal alignment of the text.
- Format text in the table just like you would any other text, although you probably will find PowerPoint's table layouts so nice that you won't need to do this!
- Hover your mouse cursor at the right edge of a column until it turns into a double-headed arrow. Then double-click to size the column automatically.
- Adjust internal cell margins using the Table Tools Layout tab, then select Alignment, Cell Margins.
- Add shading for specific rows using the check boxes in the Table Tools Design tab, Table Style Options group.

Step 7.   Use Quick Styles to Create Great-looking Charts

Office 2007 includes some beautiful charting options, and they're so easy to create and modify.

If you are following the makeover step by step, continue using your saved presentation. If you just stepped in, you can use the `medical_07.pptx` presentation from the `Makeover 02\Steps` folder on the CD.

Because this presentation was originally created in PowerPoint 2003, it uses the old MSGraph style charts. Before we can use PowerPoint 2007's formatting tools, we have to convert the old-style chart to a new one. We'll show you how you can do that and more; just follow these steps:

1. Simply double-click the chart on Slide 6, and PowerPoint will prompt you to convert the chart to the 2007 format (see Figure 3.25).

CAUTION

You must have Excel 2007 installed to access the new charting options. If you installed PowerPoint 2007 without Excel 2007, you won't see any new chart improvements!

Figure 3.25

Double-clicking a chart created in a previous version of PowerPoint prompts you to edit the chart in the old MSGraph format, convert the chart to the new 2007 format, or convert all charts in the presentation to the new 2007 format.

2. Now select the chart, and the new Chart Tools tabs—Design, Layout, and Format—become available on the Ribbon.

3. To change the chart to a 2D column, which is easier to read and displays the data more accurately than a 3D chart, click the edge of the chart to select it.

4. Click the Chart Tools Design tab, and then select Change Chart Type to bring up the dialog box that you can see in Figure 3.26.

5. Click the Clustered Column icon (the first icon in the Column category).

6. Click OK.

NOTE

You can change the chart type for just one data series. For example, you could change just one data series into a line by selecting that data series and then choosing the Chart Tools Design tab, Change Chart Type, or by right-clicking the data series and choosing Change Series Chart Type. Either of these methods opens the Change Chart Type dialog box, but applies the change only to the single data series. You can see why it's important to select the appropriate element, the entire chart, or a specific data series *before* you change the chart type.

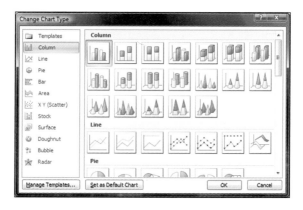

Figure 3.26

The Change Chart Type dialog box is the same dialog box that opens when you select the Insert tab on the Ribbon, and then Chart, to create a new chart.

TIP

The most often used settings for chart elements are available directly from the Chart Tools Design tab. However, it can take a lot of clicks to open the Format dialog box if you need to tweak various chart elements. Luckily, this dialog box can be accessed on the right-click menu as well. For example, right-click an axis on your chart and choose Format Axis to open the Format Axis dialog box.

Format the chart using the Chart Styles quick styles gallery on the Chart Tools Design tab. These make it easy to add flair to your charts with a single click.

1. Select the chart.

2. Click the Chart Tools Design tab on the Ribbon, and then select Chart Styles, Style 26.

To further improve the look of the chart, adjust the major unit of the vertical axis so that there are not so many numbers cluttering up the slide.

1. Click the Chart Tools Layout tab on the Ribbon, and then select Axes, Primary Vertical Axis, More Primary Vertical Axis Options.

2. In the Format Axis dialog box, click the Axis Options tab. Change the Major unit to Fixed and change 5.0 to `10.0` (see Figure 3.27).

Figure 3.27
The Format Axis dialog box lets you tweak the scale of the axis and perform a variety of other formatting tasks.

3. While you're in the Format Axis dialog box, remove the tickmarks from the axis by selecting None in both the Major and Minor tick mark type drop-down boxes. (Many presenters will

insist you keep the tickmarks. If that's the case, then leave them in, although the chart will be much cleaner without them and they're usually not really necessary.)

4. Click Close, press the Tab key, or select another option in the dialog box to apply the change.

TIP

If you prefer to have gridlines on your charts (you generally don't need them, especially if you add data labels to your charts), you can at least format them so that they're not so distracting. Simply right-click a gridline or an axis, choose Format Gridlines, and change the color to something more similar to the background or increase the transparency. To remove the gridlines, simply select them and press the Delete key, or right-click and choose Delete from the shortcut menu.

To complete the chart formatting, do the following:

1. Delete the gridlines.

2. Remove the tickmarks from the horizontal axis.

3. Right-click a column to select the data series and choose Add Data Labels. Repeat for the next column.

4. Right-click the data labels for the Chewaway series and choose Format Data Labels. Then click Label Options and choose Inside End to reposition the data labels. Repeat for the Placebo series data labels.

5. Right-click the edge of the chart to select the entire chart, and then choose 16 from the Font Size drop-down list on the mini toolbar.

6. Click and drag the right edge of the plot area so that the legend has room to breathe.

7. Click and drag to move the legend flush with the top of the chart.

8. Insert a less-than-or-equal-to symbol in the P-value text.

TIP

The less-than-or-equal-to symbol in the P-Value text box was created by typing the less-than character and formatting with an underline. Replace this cheesy text with a real symbol! With your cursor in a text box, choose the Insert tab on the Ribbon, and then click Symbol. Find the less-than-or-equal-to symbol, and click Insert. The same goes for the greater-than-or-equal-to symbol.

---

9. Unbold the text on the vertical axis title. Click and drag to center the axis title on the vertical axis.

10. Save the presentation. You can see the finished presentation in the `Makeover 02\Steps` folder on the CD (see **medical_07.pptx**).

Figure 3.28 shows you the chart prior to the formatting changes. Not very appealing, is it? Figure 3.29 shows you how you can dramatically improve the look of a chart, and of the presentation overall, with just a few clicks.

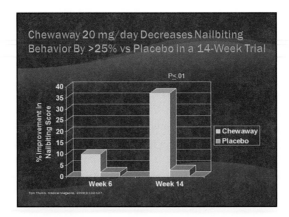

Figure 3.28
This chart, created in PowerPoint 2003, is not appealing at all.

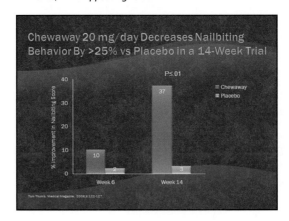

Figure 3.29
PowerPoint's new chart styles create beautiful charts with just a couple clicks.

CHARTS AND GRAPHS: BEST PRACTICES

Many presentations include a huge number of graphs. Rules of thumb include the following:

- Use consistent colors. If you can, try to use the same color for the same data throughout the presentation. For example, in this presentation, make Chewaway blue on all charts and Placebo red. If you have two doses of a compound, consider using a darker shade or lighter tint of the color for the second dosage. For example, use dark blue for Chewaway 100 mg/day and light blue for Chewaway 50 mg/day.

- Use 2D graphs, not 3D. 2D graphs show data more accurately than 3D graphs.

- Use the correct type of chart for the point you're trying to make. If in doubt, consult books like *Say It With Charts* (Gene Zelazny).

- Keep the horizontal axes aligned from chart to chart; this keeps the charts from jumping as you move from slide to slide. In addition, it goes without saying (but we'll say it anyway!) that if you have more than one chart on a slide, make sure the horizontal axes are aligned.

- Keep the vertical area of the charts the same size, even if the vertical axes have different scales.

- Make sure the slide background doesn't interfere with the data. If the background overshadows the chart and data, consider filling the plot area with a solid or semitransparent color. This can help make the data pop, so you might want to do it even if the background isn't interfering.

- Make sure lines are thick enough to be seen on line charts.

- Use symbols (such as the less-than-or-equal-to example given in the previous tip) rather than hacking something together with keyboard keys.

These simple rules will help keep your charts clean, streamlined, and professional in appearance.

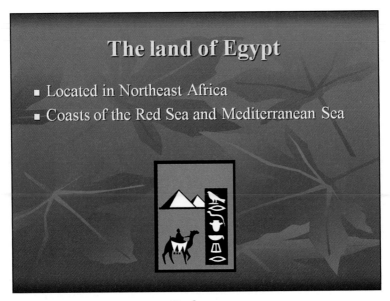

Before

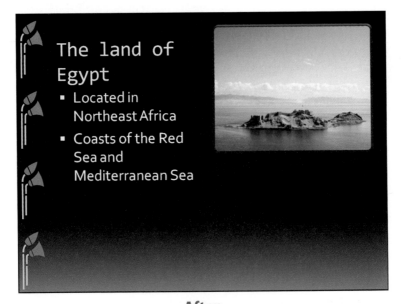

After

ON THE CD:

The sample presentation and all other files with which you need to work can be found on the CD in the `Makeover 03` folder.

4

Makeover 3: School Project

YOU WILL LEARN HOW TO:

- Apply and Edit Themes
- Make Presentations Aesthetic
- Add Pictures
- Add Picture Effects
- Compress Pictures

About This Makeover

Many schools all over the United States and other countries use PowerPoint to make their respective subjects interesting. Thus, if the class is learning photosynthesis in the science class, the teacher shows them a PowerPoint presentation on the subject. More often than not, these presentations are created by the teachers or by the students as a school project.

School presentations created in PowerPoint face unique problems. First of all, resources usually are not available to hire professional designers to create artwork. Even if the designers could be hired, it might not be a good thing to do because teachers and students learn so much about PowerPoint while they are creating these presentations. In addition, the object of creating presentations sometimes is to help build team spirit.

Another aspect of school presentations is that they are rarely sold, or even shown to audiences other than the students and teachers. This in turn makes them a great platform on which to experiment—and sometimes these experiments can go awry. We've often seen school presentations that use a different background for every slide!

The makeover for this chapter is a typical school presentation. In this chapter, we take an existing school project presentation on the Egyptian civilization and make it more aesthetic.

The pre-makeover presentation uses some clip art that is neither consistent nor contemporary. The slide background, fonts, and layout look like they were created in PowerPoint 4 or 95—more than a decade ago. Looks like the creators of this presentation took their "Egyptian civilization" topic a little too seriously and made the presentation look positively ancient!

Figure 4.1 shows you the "before" sample slides. They were created in an older version of PowerPoint, and then some edits were made in PowerPoint 2007.

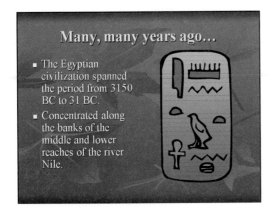 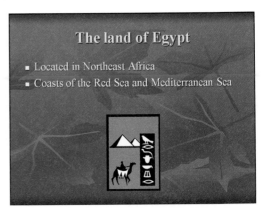

Figure 4.1

Functional, yet missing any pizzazz.

Figure 4.2 shows the "after" sample slides with a few changes that made a huge impact.

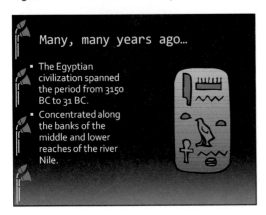 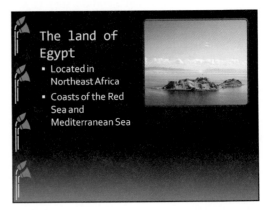

Figure 4.2

Changes in color, layout, and pictures can make the same slide look so much better.

Step 1. Apply and Edit Themes

Before you start this makeover, do a little research and find out which colors the ancient Egyptians used. We searched a few online resources, looked at several printed books, and decided that a black background with some turquoise blue and golden yellow would look the best.

Based on these observations, we chose an existing PowerPoint 2007 theme and edited the theme to create the look we wanted. You'll learn more about this process as you progress through this chapter.

Apply the Theme to the Entire Presentation

Let's start by applying a new theme:

1. Open the `egypt_00.pptx` presentation from the `Makeover 03\Steps` folder on the CD.

2. Click the Design tab on the Ribbon, and click the down arrow in the Themes group to open the Theme gallery, as shown in Figure 4.3.

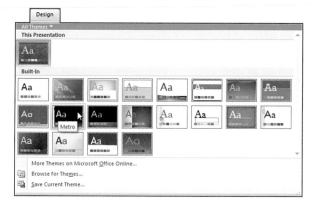

Figure 4.3

Changing a theme can metamorphose your PowerPoint presentations.

3. Select the theme called Metro by clicking it. This theme now is applied to the entire presentation. Save your presentation.

Although this theme does look contemporary, it still needs an Egyptian look. That's simple enough to do.

Change the Border

If you look closely, you'll find that every slide has a thin, white border on the left side. We'll get rid of this border and replace it with a suitable Egyptian ornamental border. So, where do you get a border? That's quite easy—search for some ornamental designs on Microsoft's Office Online site or design your own border, if you know how to create your own designs in a graphics program.

To make things easier for you, we included a border design in the `Makeover 03\Pictures` folder of the CD; the design is in a file called **border.emf**.

1. Click the View tab on the Ribbon, and click the Slide Master button to get into Slide Master view, as shown in Figure 4.4.

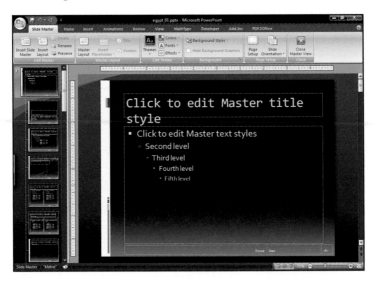

Figure 4.4

Editing themes in Slide Master view.

2. Select the first (larger) thumbnail in the left pane to select the Slide Master, and then place your cursor a little outside the slide area in the top left of the main workspace. Now drag your cursor all the way to the bottom of the slide (see Figure 4.5) so that you select every element in the white border. Press the Delete key on your keyboard. If you find that some of the border elements were not deleted, select them individually and delete them.

    You might find that the first layout thumbnail below the Slide Master (the Title Slide Layout) still has that white border. Select that layout in the left pane, and remove the border for this layout (as explained previously for the Slide Master).

3. Select the first (larger) thumbnail in the left pane again to select the Slide Master. Now click the Insert tab on the Ribbon, and click the Picture option. This brings up the Insert Picture dialog box. Navigate to the Pictures subfolder in the `Makeover 03` folder (see Figure 4.6), and select the **border.emf** graphic. Click Insert to get back to the Slide Master.

Figure 4.5

Drag a marquee to quickly select multiple objects.

Figure 4.6

Insert the Egyptian border.

4. By default, the border is placed in the center of the slide. Drag the border to the left, and resize or reposition as required. Figure 4.7 shows the border after we finished placing and resizing it.

Select this border, copy it, and paste it into the Title Slide Layout (which is the one immediately below the large Slide Master thumbnail in the left pane).

Figure 4.7

The new border is on the slide.

5. Click the Slide Master tab on the Ribbon, and click the Close button.

6. Save your presentation.

Step 2. Edit the First Slide

We know that we want to add better pictures to the slides. However, I do like the graphics on Slides 3 and 5 and want to retain them. When you look closely, they look almost like a set.

The first edit here is to move these graphics from their existing slides to the first slide. If you are fol-lowing the makeover step by step, continue using your saved presentation. If you just stepped in, you can use the `eqypt_01.pptx` presentation from the `Makeover 03\Steps` folder on the CD.

1. Select the graphic on slide 3, and press Ctrl+X to cut it. Click slide 1, and paste the graphic by pressing Ctrl+V. Do the same thing with the graphic on slide 5. Reposition both graphics on slide 1 so that they appear as shown in Figure 4.8.

2. Select both graphics, and click the Picture Tools Format tab on the Ribbon. Click the down arrow in the Picture Styles group, as shown in Figure 4.9, and select the Reflected Bevel, Black option.

3. Save the presentation.

Figure 4.8
Moving graphics to slide 1.

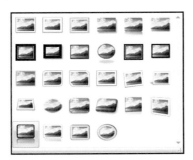

Figure 4.9
Adding picture effects.

Step 3. Add Some Pictures, Add Some Effects

We now will add some pictures to the slides. Then we can add effects to those pictures. If you are following the makeover step by step, continue using your saved presentation. If you just stepped in, you can use the **egypt_02.pptx** presentation from the Makeover 03 folder on the CD. Then, go straight to slide 4.

1. Click the Insert tab on the Ribbon, and choose Picture to open the Insert Picture dialog box. Navigate to the Pictures subfolder in the Makeover 03\Steps folder on the CD. Select the **0380045.jpg** picture, and click Insert to get back to the slide.

2. Resize the picture so that it covers a quarter of the slide area, and drag it so that it anchors to the top-right of the slide, as you can see in Figure 4.10.

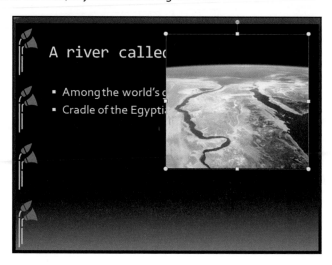

Figure 4.10

Resize and reposition the picture.

3. You'll find that the picture now covers nearly half the text area (refer to Figure 4.10). To rectify that issue, we'll have to select the title and text boxes, and then resize them by dragging the handles on the right side toward the center so that they fit on the left side of the slide, as you can see in Figure 4.11.

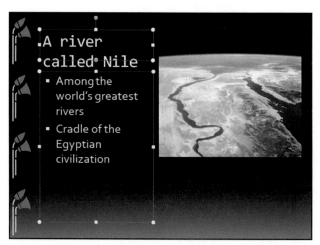

Figure 4.11

Resize the title and text boxes so that they fit on the left side of the slide.

TIP

As much as possible, avoid resizing title and text boxes. However, when you have to do it, never drag the boxes around; instead, resize them by dragging the handles in from the right side of the boxes. Never drag from the top or the left side of the boxes to resize because that alters those important margins in the slide. The human eye is very perceptive of the left and top margins, but quite forgiving with changes in the bottom and right margins.

4. Select the picture, and then click the Picture Tools Format tab on the Ribbon. Bring up the Picture Styles gallery, as shown earlier in this chapter in Figure 4.9, and select the Reflected Bevel, Black option.

5. There are a few more pictures in the `Makeover 03\Pictures` folder on the CD that you can insert in the remaining slides. In addition, make sure you resize the pictures and text boxes as required.

6. Add effects to all inserted pictures.

7. Save your presentation.

We had a few extra pictures that went well with the subject of this presentation. We added them to an extra slide at the end of this presentation (see Figure 4.12). These pictures have been provided courtesy of PhotoSpin.com. Check out their site for many more photos, illustrations, fonts, and the so on.

We also inserted a few images from PowerPoint's Clip Art task pane (see the following Tip).

TIP

PowerPoint includes its own amazing gallery of clip art and pictures. To access these, make sure you are online, click the Insert tab on the Ribbon, and then click the Clip Art task pane, which lets you search and insert visuals on your slides.

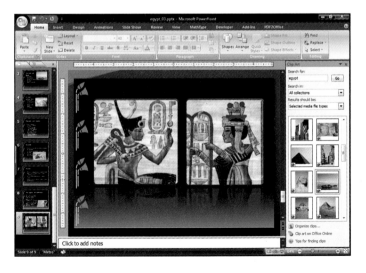

Figure 4.12

Let the pictures create an aura.

Step 4. Compress Your Presentation

It's easy to add pictures to your PowerPoint presentations. And it's even easier to insert photos that have been shot with multi-megapixel digital cameras that create 5 megabyte images! When you insert these images, however, the file size of the presentation can balloon miserably!

Fortunately, there is a quick fix. If you are following the makeover step by step, continue using your saved presentation. If you just stepped in, you can use the `egypt_03.pptx` presentation from the `Makeover 03\Steps` folder on the CD.

Follow these steps:

1. Go to any slide that includes a picture. Select the picture.

2. Click the Picture Tools Format tab on the Ribbon, and click the Compress Images option to bring up the Compress Pictures dialog box, as shown in Figure 4.13.

Figure 4.13
Streamline oversized pictures using the Compress Pictures tool.

3. Make sure the Apply to selected pictures only check box is not checked, and then click the Options button to bring up the Compression Settings dialog box, as shown in Figure 4.14.

Figure 4.14
Choose your compression settings.

4. Match the compression settings to those you see in Figure 4.14, and click OK. Click OK again to apply the settings.

5. Save your presentation.

The finished presentation, **egypt_04.pptx**, is on the `Makeover 03\Steps` folder on the CD.

You'll notice that even after compression, the file size has reduced by a mere 1 KB! That's because PowerPoint 2007 automatically performs basic compression when you save a file. Most of the time, this automatic compression works very well, but if you want to do the compression manually, you know how you can do that by following the steps explained in this chapter.

More Case Studies: Summary

		Client 3	Client 4	Client 5
Work Period		3 Years	6 Years	5 Years
Satisfaction	Liaison	Retained	Retained	Improved
	PR and Media			Retained
Future Prospects		Awesome, company has several new plans	No change in status	Dim

Before

More Case Studies: Summary

		Client 3	Client 4	Client 5
Work Period		3 Years	6 Years	5 Years
Satisfaction	Liaison	Retained	Retained	Improved
	PR and Media			Retained
Future Prospects		Awesome, company has several new plans	No change in status	Dim

After

Makeover 4:
A Group Presentation

YOU WILL LEARN HOW TO:

- Reapply Slide Layouts
- Prune Slide Content
- Work with Table Tools
- Work with Incomplete Slides
- Make Slides Look Consistent
- Use PowerPoint's Drop-down Galleries

About This Makeover

So, what is a group presentation? A group presentation is one in which more than one presenter is involved and the slides contained in the presentation file come from disparate sources. Typically, the presentations contain these slides:

- A cover slide
- A section cover slide for every presenter
- Other slides for each presenter

Many times, this sort of presentation is cooked up by combining the slides of all presenters just before the session. It ends up resembling a hot bowl of soup with vegetable pieces that look very different—you have carrots in the soup, but some carrots are cut round, some are small pieces, and some are julienne! Needless to say, the person drinking this soup (or the audience member seeing this presentation) will be none too pleased. Fortunately, you can make your presentation slides consistent, even if the actual slides came from disparate sources!

This group presentation has slides from three presentations that were merged at the last minute because three presenters were taking part.

Normally, such presentations comprise many more slides, but we retained a few typical slide types so that you get an idea of how to approach this sort of makeover.

This makeover doesn't include many changes to color or the addition of many visuals because we know that, typically, there is not much time provided to do these last-minute makeovers. Thus, in this makeover, we'll apply a new theme, make some small changes, and show you how to make things work, even with incomplete slides.

Figure 5.1 shows you the "before" sample slides. These were assembled in PowerPoint 2007 using one of PowerPoint's built-in themes. Even then, it's easy to go wrong! Remember, even though these slides were assembled in PowerPoint 2007, it's entirely possible that they were originally created in earlier versions of PowerPoint. And because that is something you will face so often, it's great that you get to work with such a mish-mash in this makeover.

Figure 5.2 shows our "after" sample slides with minimal color and theme changes, but as you can see, the makeover does provide an amazing change. In addition, the best part is that we created no new theme and inserted no new pictures. Everything done here was done with what's available in every copy of PowerPoint 2007!

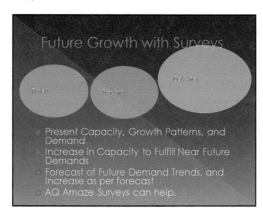

Figure 5.1

Slides victimized by the wrong colors.

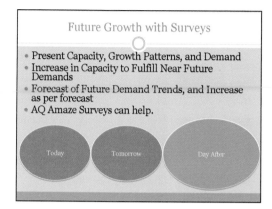

Figure 5.2

Slides reborn with some quick makeover tricks.

Step 1. Reapply Slide Layouts

Before we get started with this presentation, open the presentation itself, and take a look at the slides. To get the full effect, you need to look at every slide in the presentation all the way through to the end. It's easy to notice that the slides themselves have so much to dislike: The text placeholders are not properly aligned, the table uses colors that can make you sick, and there are no visuals in the slides. In fact, some of the slides contain too much text.

Now look at the slides again, but try to look at things that are similar in the slides. It's a wonder that you can even find content that is similar in such inconsistent slides, but if you look hard, we're sure you'll notice a few things. They include text boxes, section slides, and similar layouts.

The trick in this makeover is to use the similar elements in various slides to bind the entire presentation—even an inconsistent presentation like this one—with consistency.

The first thing you need to do is to reapply the layouts. Remember, at this point, we are not applying another theme; we are working with the layouts from the original presentation and just making sure it's been properly applied to all the slides in this motley assortment of slides. Let's get started now:

1. Open the `amaze_00.pptx` presentation from the `Makeover 04\Steps` folder on the CD. Make sure you are on the first slide of the presentation.

2. Click the Home tab on the Ribbon, and click the Layout option to view the Layout gallery, as shown in Figure 5.3.

Figure 5.3
Changing layouts.

3. Apply available layouts to the slides by clicking the layout thumbnail in the Layout gallery. Apply the layouts to the slides as follows:

- Title Slide layout: slides 1, 3, 8, 12, and 17
- Title Only layout: slide 11
- Title and Content layout: slides 2, 4–7, 9, 10, and 13–16

4. Now click the View tab on the Ribbon, and click Slide Sorter so that you can see thumbnails of all slides. Press Ctrl+A to select all slides in the presentation. In the Home tab on the Ribbon, click the Reset button.

5. Click the View tab on the Ribbon, and click Normal. Save your presentation.

Step 2. Choose a New Theme

Although the theme applied in this presentation is an original PowerPoint 2007 theme, we must say that there are better themes provided within PowerPoint.

It's easy to apply a new theme to an existing presentation. Choosing the right one to apply, however, takes more effort. These guidelines will help:

- Try previewing all themes in the Theme gallery. You can find the Theme gallery in the Design tab on the Ribbon. To preview themes, select a bulleted slide or a title slide, and hover over the thumbnails in the Themes gallery to see a live preview to see how your slide will look without actually applying the theme.

TIP

Can't see any live previews? They might be turned off. To turn them on, choose Office Button, then PowerPoint Options. Be sure the Enable Live Preview option is checked.

- Even if no theme pleases you, choose one that is close to the result you want. Later, you can edit the theme to make it more suitable.

- Try to look for third-party themes; you'll find a list on this book's companion site, http://www.pptkit.com/morethemes/.

Now that we have given you some food for thought, you can apply a new theme to your presentation. If you are following the makeover step by step, continue using your saved presentation. If you just stepped in, you can use the **amaze_01.pptx** presentation from the `Makeover 04\Steps` folder on the CD.

1. Click the Design tab on the Ribbon, and click the down arrow in the Themes group to view the Themes gallery (see Figure 5.4).

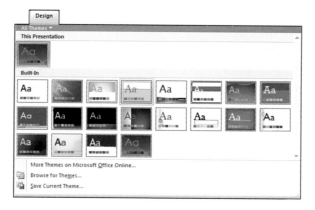

Figure 5.4

Applying a new theme.

2. We chose the Civic theme because it's got a nice, clean look. This sort of look can work in almost any situation.

TIP

White backgrounds are good to use with presentations that have pictures and visuals that contain a variety of colors.

3. View the presentation, and you'll find the following problem areas:
    - Too much text in some of the slides
    - Non-standard fonts (not based on the applied theme) in some slides

- A terrible table in one of the slides
- Problem areas in the Future Growth and Contact slides

4. We'll tackle these issues in the rest of this makeover. For now, save the presentation.

Step 3. Prune Text and Add New Slides

It's easy to understand why slides have so much text. Overly enthusiastic presenters tend to do the following:

- Copy and paste paragraphs from other company content, such as text from a brochure or website.
- Write long, long sentences so that the slides look busy; they think that this is a reflection of their great skills.
- Cram everything onto a slide so they won't forget something important—or even something not so important!
- Use PowerPoint like a word processor.

Well, those are the more common reasons, but the main reason is that people don't realize that PowerPoint is a different medium altogether and it needs to be looked at with a different perspective. Luckily, you are reading this book, and we'll share the secrets with you. Keep reading!

Pruning Text

If you are following the makeover step by step, continue using your saved presentation. If you just stepped in, you can use the `amaze_02.pptx` presentation from the `Makeover 04\Steps` folder on the CD.

1. The first four slides are fine. Go straight to the fifth slide.

2. Do you see all the gobbledygook on this slide? Why use the barrage of sentences when a few direct phrases will provide the same information?

So how do you approach this task? Let's examine the first paragraph on this slide (look at the slide on the left in Figure 5.5). We can easily change that long epic to just two bullets:

- Developed as a separate division in 1987
- To provide liaison, PR, and survey skills

Keep pruning your sentences to more direct phrases that get the attention of the audience. That's the reason these phrases are called bullets—they demand and get attention!

3. In the same way, we pruned the other sentences to bullets. Figure 5.5 shows the results for the fifth slide.

4. Save the presentation.

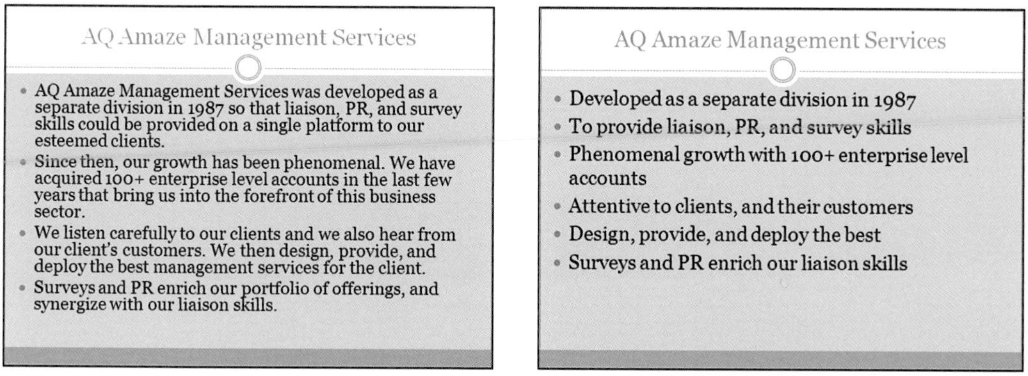

Figure 5.5

A more direct slide.

TIP

As a rule of the thumb, direct phrases on slides don't end with a period but sentences do. Alternatively, leave ending punctuation off bulleted text altogether, whether it's a phrase or a sentence—the punctuation needlessly clutters the slide. However, be consistent with whichever approach you prefer.

Adding New Slides

Now move to slide 6. Even if we were to clean up this slide, it still would be crowded with content. In addition, you'll have to keep the font point size really small to cram everything in. When faced with a situation like this, you can take one of two approaches:

- Ask the presenter if some of the content can be removed.
- Ask the presenter if the slide content can be divided to create two slides.

For this makeover, we're taking the latter approach.

To divide the content of an overcrowded slide, you should not divide the bullets and merely place them in successive slides. As much as possible, you should retain related bullets together on the same slide. Try to divide the bullets into two or more topic areas; this is not as difficult as it may sound.

TIP

It's a good idea to check with the presenter when reorganizing bullet points on slides. Sometimes the order of the bulleted text is important to them.

Let's take slide 6 for instance. We rearranged the bullets and split the slide content into two slides.

Follow these steps to reorganize a slide that contains too much text:

1. Make sure you are on slide 6 (see Figure 5.6).

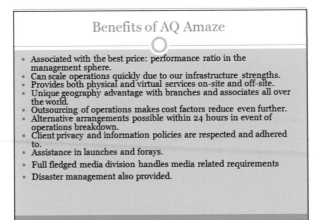

Before

Figure 5.6

The original slide jammed full of text.

2. Cut the third bullet (Ctrl+X) and paste it into position below the ninth bullet (Ctrl+V) so that you move this bullet to the second-to-last position. We do this because the content in the third bullet seemed related to the text in the ninth bullet.

3. Right-click slide 6 in the Slides pane, and choose Duplicate Slide. This creates two incarnations of the slide at slide 6 and slide 7 positions.

4. Delete the last five bullets in slide 6. Similarly, delete the first five bullets in slide 7. PowerPoint automatically increases the font size of the bullet text.

5. Because none of the bullets actually comprise sentences, remove the periods at the end of each phrase.

6. Suffix the title in slide 7 with the word `(cont.)` or `(cont'd.)`. At this point, your slides should look like the after slides in Figure 5.7.

7. Save the presentation.

TIP

Remember that from now on, all slide numbers after slide 6 changed because an extra slide is inserted. Also, we added "cont'd." in the title of slide 7 so that the audience knows that this is a continued slide.

You can also make the word "cont'd" smaller than the title text if you have a really long title and are running out of space

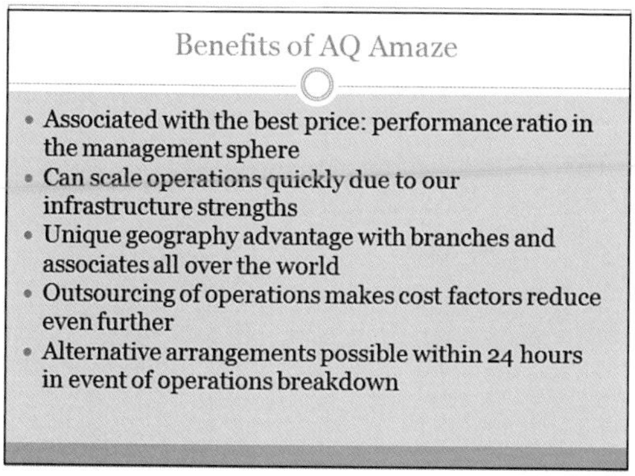

Benefits of AQ Amaze

- Associated with the best price: performance ratio in the management sphere
- Can scale operations quickly due to our infrastructure strengths
- Unique geography advantage with branches and associates all over the world
- Outsourcing of operations makes cost factors reduce even further
- Alternative arrangements possible within 24 hours in event of operations breakdown

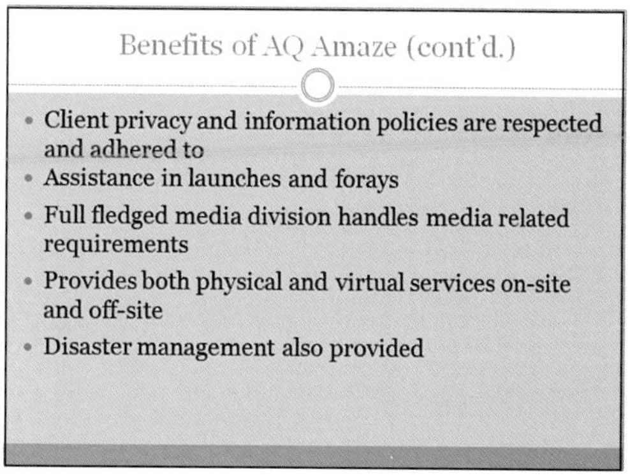

Benefits of AQ Amaze (cont'd.)

- Client privacy and information policies are respected and adhered to
- Assistance in launches and forays
- Full fledged media division handles media related requirements
- Provides both physical and virtual services on-site and off-site
- Disaster management also provided

After

Figure 5.7

Splitting the content and adding a slide.

Step 4. Add the Footnotes

When we changed the theme earlier in this makeover, the font type in the footers contained in slides 8, 11, and 16 did not change. They did not change because those footers were not formatted to follow the active Theme Fonts.

Fortunately, there is a quick fix. If you are following the makeover step by step, continue using your saved presentation. If you just stepped in, you can use the `amaze_03.pptx` presentation from the `Makeover 04\Steps` folder on the CD.

Follow these steps:

1. Go straight to the eighth slide.

2. Select the footer, and make sure that the Home tab on the Ribbon is visible.

3. Then, click the Font list arrow to view the font choices in a drop-down list shown in Figure 5.8.

4. In this drop-down list, you'll find the Theme Fonts right on top. Click the Theme Font style that says Body (refer to Figure 5.8). Change the font size to 16, non-bold.

5. Repeat the same process for the footer in slide 11 and in slide 16.

6. Next, you'll need to make sure that the position of the footers in slides 8, 11, and 16 is consistent. Select the footer in slide 8, right-click and choose Size and Position to bring up a dialog box of the same name. You'll find the position coordinates in the suitably named Position tab that you can see in Figure 5.9. Change these position coordinates to Horizontal (`0.44`") and Vertical (`7`"), as shown in Figure 5.9.

Figure 5.8
Change the Theme Font.

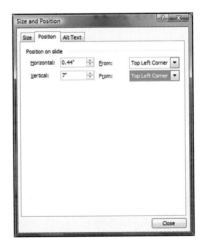

Figure 5.9
Copy position coordinates to other slide footers.

7. With the Size and Position dialog box still floating over the slide area, navigate to slides 11 and 16 one after the other, select the footers, and change their position coordinates to match the ones for the footer in slide 8.

8. Click Close to get an uncluttered view of your slide.

TIP

You could include a footer placeholder in the Slide Master itself so that it shows up on all slides. Then delete it from the slides you don't want a footer on. That way they are all in the same position on each slide. However, because the goal here is to put together some slides quickly, you can make do with the Size and Position dialog box.

---

9. Save the presentation.

Step 5. A Table Overhaul

If you are following this makeover from the previous step, open your presentation. Alternatively, open the `amaze_04.pptx` presentation from the `Makeover 04\Steps` folder on the CD, and look at the table on slide 12.

Wow—isn't the table on slide 12 a visual definition of the word horrendous? It is something that I would call a design agency's worst nightmare. However, PowerPoint 2007 can metamorphose this ugly duckling into a beautiful swan with just a few clicks!

Follow these steps to learn some table wizardry:

1. Go straight to the twelfth slide.

2. Select the table, and you'll see that the Ribbon area has two new tabs within the Table Tools category: the Design tab and the Layout tab.

3. Click the Table Tools Design tab. Then, in the Table Styles area, click the More arrow to view the Table Styles drop-down gallery, which you can see in Figure 5.10.

4. You can hover over any of these thumbnails to activate Live Preview to see how the changes look on your table. However, because the Table Styles gallery is so large, you might see the Live Preview on only a part of your table unless you have a high-resolution display.

TIP

You can also scroll through the thumbnails in the Table Styles gallery without using it as a drop-down gallery—this shows the Live Preview. To navigate between the thumbnails in the gallery use the up and down arrow keys to the right of the gallery.

---

5. We like the Themed Style 1 – Accent 3 option. Choose that table style and apply it to the table (see Figure 5.11).

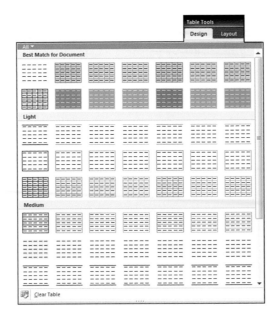

Figure 5.10

Give your table a new life.

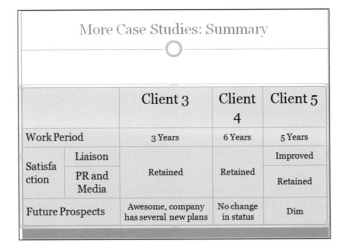

Figure 5.11

The new look still needs fine-tuning.

6. Now drag the vertical line to the right of the cell that contains the word "Satisfaction" so that the entire word fits in one line. Then, drag the line between the first and second columns so that the word "Liaison" fits in one line rather than splitting it up in two lines (see Figure 5.12).

7. Now select the last three columns in the table. As you can see, they are not evenly sized. With the columns selected, click the Table Tools Layout tab on the Ribbon. Within the Cell Size group, click the Distribute Columns option, as shown in Figure 5.12.

Figure 5.12 also shows you the result of distributing the columns evenly.

8. Save the presentation.

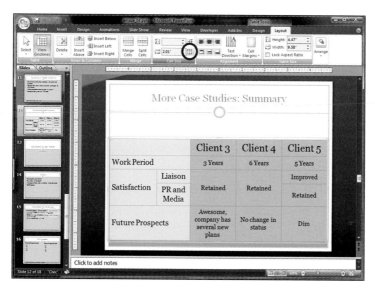

Figure 5.12
One click to equality.

Step 6. Fix Those Incomplete Slides

Every company has folks who are either too busy or too lazy. They don't want to do anything until the last minute, and the third presenter in our group presentation—Dan Klipkoos—is one of them! His slides look like a hurried, five-minute job. His reasoning is that he'll add the content after the presentation has been through the makeover that the design agency is doing!

So, yes, you could fret and insist that Dan send the content now, but that won't help. Therefore, in this section, we'll show you how you can work with incomplete slides.

If you are following the makeover step by step, continue using your saved presentation. If you just stepped in, you can use the `amaze_05.pptx` presentation from the `Makeover 04\Steps` folder on the CD. In the presentation, you will see that slides 15, 16, and 17 are incomplete in some way or the other.

1. First, let's tackle slide 15. Select the three ovals, and press the down-arrow key on your keyboard until the oval shapes are below the text placeholder.

2. With the three shapes still selected, click the Drawing Tools Format tab on the Ribbon, and in the Align group, choose Align Middle (see the result in Figure 5.13). Choose Align, Distribute Horizontally.

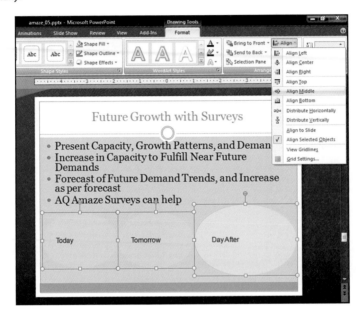

Figure 5.13
Align oval shapes in a row.

3. Now select the first two shapes in the slide, click the Drawing Tools Format tab, and click the More arrow in the Shapes Style group to access the Shape Styles gallery. Choose a contrasting color style that stands out on the slide background. We chose Light 1 Outline, Colored Fill – Accent 1 (this is the second option in the third row within the gallery).

4. Now choose the last shape and apply another Shape Style to this one. We chose Light 1 Outline, Colored Fill – Accent 5 (this is the sixth option in the third row within the gallery). You'll notice that applying a Shape Style also changes the font style in the shapes to the Theme Font.

5. We also can make the text on this slide take up less space by reducing the text font size. Select all the text in the placeholder, and press Ctrl+Shift+< to reduce the font size. Now if the presenter wants to add some captions to the ovals or add some more shapes, he'll have room on the slide to do that.

With the text still selected, we pressed Ctrl+E to center the text in the ovals. Your slide should now look like what you see in Figure 5.14.

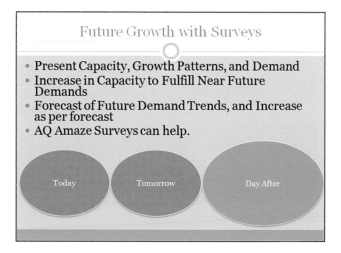

Figure 5.14

Perfect alignment and contrast make an aesthetic difference.

TIP

It's easy to use shortcut keys like Ctrl+E to center text rather than accessing the options on the Ribbon or the mini toolbar. Learn these shortcut keys, and your productivity will soar. Also, you can press Ctrl+L to left justify and Ctrl+R to right justify text.

---

6. Save the presentation, and move on to slide 16. This slide has no real text content for the bullets, but the presenter clearly intends to add something. Leave this for now, and proceed to slide 17.

7. Slide 17 has a typical problem. The text content is very much there, but it's not contained within the default text placeholder—someone put it in another text box. Select the text in the text box (from "Contact Us" to "Web") and copy the text. Then, delete the text box altogether, and paste the copied text into the placeholder (where it says "Click to add text"). You'll see a smart tag immediately after you paste; make sure that you select the Use Destination Theme option, as you can see in Figure 5.15.

Notice that there's an extra space before the text "Email" and "Phone." Delete those extra spaces.

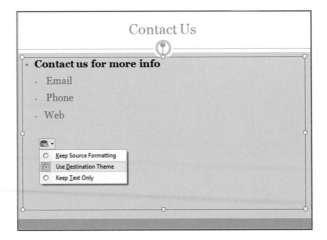

Figure 5.15

Add the text to the placeholder.

8. Still on slide 17, notice that one of the bullets is in bold, quite opposite the norm for the rest of the slides. To correct this, just make sure that slide 17 is active, click the Home tab on the Ribbon, and click the Reset button. This makes the slide look consistent with the rest of the slides.

9. We are almost done with this presentation, but it is a good idea to remind the presenter that some slides are incomplete.

   To do that, go to slide 16. Click the Insert tab on the Ribbon, choose the Text Box option, and draw a small box on the slide. Type a message, maybe something like "This slide is incomplete," inside the text box.

10. Now drag this box to the top-right portion of the slide. With the box still selected, click the Drawing Tools Format tab, access the Shape Styles gallery, and choose a style that really contrasts with the rest of the slide so that it draws the attention of the presenter, as shown in Figure 5.16.

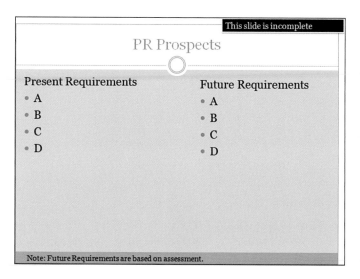

Figure 5.16

Add a note to the presenter in the incomplete slide.

11. Copy the text box, and paste it in the other incomplete slides.

TIP

Rather than use an attention-grabbing text box, you can use PowerPoint's Comments feature to mark some slides as incomplete. You'll find Comments in the Review tab on the Ribbon.

We think comments are not as noticeable as "screaming" text boxes, but one benefit is they don't show up unexpectedly in Slide Show View. Ultimately, the purpose of these notes is to warn the presenter that these slides need some input. Just to be sure, do include a paper note or send an email to the presenter and let them know these slides are incomplete.

---

12. Save the presentation.

You can see the completed file by opening **amaze_06.pptx** presentation from the Makeover 04\Steps folder on the CD.

Before

After

Makeover 5:
Halloween Scrapbook

About This Makeover

This Halloween theme presentation is accompanied by some scary music. The Halloween party organizers will play it for partygoers just before they announce the awards for the best costumes.

This was so much fun to work with. The original presentation contained several slides with pictures, but it did not use the new Slide Layouts option to create several picture layout slides.

In addition, this was intended to be a scrapbook-style presentation, but there were no add-on elements, such as buttons or ornaments, to provide that scrapbook "look," so we used an assortment of coordinated, add-on picture elements to make the presentation look more like an electronic scrapbook.

Check out the before and after sample, and then follow us as we lead you through this eerie world of ghosts, goblins, bats, and pumpkins!

Figure 6.1 shows you the "before" slides. These were created in PowerPoint 2007 using one of PowerPoint's built-in themes. The theme used in this presentation was a slightly modified version of Trek, which is one of the better themes bundled with PowerPoint. However, as you can see, the theme presents an almost joyful atmosphere to the slides, which is quite unlike a typical Halloween theme that can be identified by a scary, dark look.

YOU WILL LEARN HOW TO:

- Change Backgrounds
- Create and Apply Theme Fonts
- Format Text
- Create Slide Layouts
- Add Theme Colors
- Include Add-on Elements
- Add Scary Music

Figure 6.1

Halloween looks happy, not scary.

Figure 6.2 shows our "after" slides. These slides have the same text and the same pictures; it's just that a new theme makes them look eerie and more Halloween-like in appearance. Just wait until you hear the scary music we added!

Figure 6.2

Yes, that's scarier.

Step 1.   Change the Background

The first step in this makeover process is to insert a picture onto the slide background. Do note the distinction—you'll insert a picture on the *slide master*, not format the slide background, because we want to use the Recolor Picture option in PowerPoint that works only with inserted pictures.

You'll want to use a background picture that lends itself to PowerPoint's recoloring options. Most of the time, you'll want to use a grayscale image that is neither uniformly gray nor presented with too much contrast. In other words, it should contain subtle shadows and highlighted areas to look great. See Figure 6.3 to get an idea of the type of picture that makes a good background for this purpose.

You will find the background picture we have used, `halloween_back.jpg`, on the CD in the `Makeover 05\Pictures` folder (see Figure 6.3).

Figure 6.3

Black background with bats and an eerie castle tower.

Open the `halloween_00.pptx` presentation from the `Makeover 05\Steps` folder on the CD.

Follow these steps to change the background picture in the Slide Master:

1. Select the View tab on the Ribbon, and then click the Slide Master button to open Slide Master view (see Figure 6.4).

2. Select the Slide Master on the left pane; the Slide Master is the larger thumbnail on the left, whereas all the smaller thumbnails below the Slide Master are for the Slide Layouts.

3. While still in Slide Master view, click the Insert tab on the Ribbon, and then click Picture. This brings up the Insert Picture dialog box that you can see in Figure 6.5.

4. Select the `Halloween_back.jpg` picture from the `Makeover 05\Pictures` folder on the CD with this book, and then click Insert. You'll see the picture inserted within the Master.

Each Slide Master...

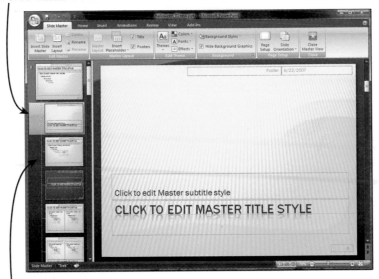

...can have several Slide Layouts

Figure 6.4

In Slide Master view.

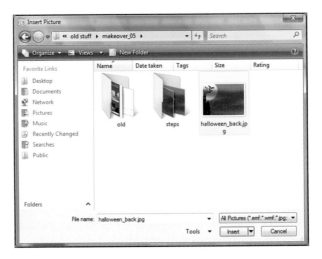

Figure 6.5

Insert a picture in the Slide Master.

5. If the inserted picture does not fill the entire slide area, select the picture and drag any of the selection handles on the picture to resize it to fit the slide area. Right-click the picture, and choose Send to Back.

6. With the picture still selected, you should see the Picture Tools Format tab on the Ribbon. Click this tab, and click the Recolor button to view the Recolor gallery shown in Figure 6.6.

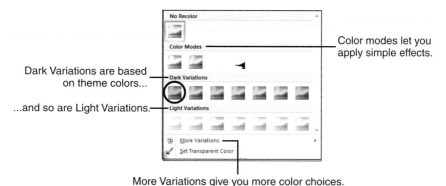

Color modes let you apply simple effects.

Dark Variations are based on theme colors...

...and so are Light Variations.

More Variations give you more color choices.

Figure 6.6

Recolor the inserted picture.

7. Choose the first recolor variation (the ToolTip shows Text color 2 Dark when you hover over it with your mouse) within the Dark Variations section.

8. Click the Slide Master tab on the Ribbon, and explore all the Slide Layouts visible under the active Slide Master, as shown in Figure 6.7. You'll see that some of them don't show your inserted Halloween picture at all!

Figure 6.7

Some slides don't show the inserted picture because the Hide Background Graphics option is checked.

9. Select the offending Slide Layout thumbnail, and uncheck the Hide Background Graphics check box in the Slide Master tab of the Ribbon (refer to Figure 6.7). Repeat the same process for all Slide Layouts so that they now sport Halloween backgrounds.

10. Click the Slide Master tab of the Ribbon, and then click the Close Master View button at the end of the Ribbon. Save your presentation.

Step 2.   Create Theme Fonts

The next step is to create a new Theme Font set for this presentation. Fortunately, it's quite easy to create a Theme Font set in PowerPoint, but first let me tell you what a Theme Font set is.

Microsoft created this new PowerPoint 2007 feature so that you can give a presentation a set of consistent font styles to apply to various slide objects (titles, body text, and so on) that all work well together rather than having a mishmash of different font types that scream unprofessional.

If you are following the makeover step by step, continue using your saved presentation. If you just stepped in, you can use the `halloween_01.pptx` presentation from the `Makeover 05\Steps` folder on the CD.

To create your own Theme Font set, follow these steps:

1. Click the Design tab on the Ribbon, and click the Fonts button to view the Fonts gallery (see Figure 6.8).

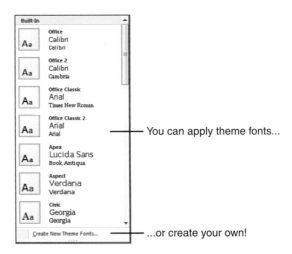

Figure 6.8

Office 2007 applications come with coordinated Theme Font sets.

2. All the existing options in this gallery are Theme Font sets that you can apply to the open presentation with one click. For now, ignore these existing Theme Font sets and choose the last option in the gallery, Create New Theme Fonts.

3. This brings up the dialog box of the same name, as you can see in Figure 6.9.

Figure 6.9

Create your own Theme Font set here!

4. Select the Heading font; for this example, I chose Tw Cen MT as the heading font within the Heading font drop-down list.

   Select the Body font; for this example, I chose Tw Cen MT Condensed as the body font within the Body font drop-down list.

   If you don't have these fonts on your system, you can use any other font that you think matches the mood of the presentation.

   Give a name to your new Theme Font set. I called mine `Halloween Fonts`, but you can choose any other name.

5. Click the Save button on the QAT (or press Ctrl + S) to save your presentation.

Step 3.   Apply Theme Fonts

After you create your own Theme Font set in PowerPoint, you can apply it to your open presentation. If you followed the previous step, PowerPoint might have actually applied the Theme Font set you created to the presentation. Even if it did that (or not), go ahead with this section of the makeover because you'll learn how you can apply an existing Theme Fonts set.

If you are following the makeover step by step, continue using your saved presentation. If you just stepped in, you can use the `halloween_02.pptx` presentation from the `Makeover 05\Steps` folder on the CD.

To apply a Theme Font set, follow these steps:

1. Click the Design tab on the Ribbon, and click the Fonts button to view the Fonts gallery that you can see in Figure 6.10.

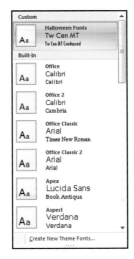

Figure 6.10

Apply a Theme Font set.

2. Click a Theme Font set within this gallery; if you created your own Theme Font sets, these should be visible here as well.

3. If you are not happy with the choice, you can opt to apply another Theme Font set, or you can press Ctrl+Z to undo the new font choice.

Step 4.   Fine-tune Your Fonts Further

Although Theme Fonts are a great feature that let you create coordinated font sets, they don't let you set other font attributes, such as bold or underline.

TIP

Do you want to make the text stay all caps? If so, select your text and head to the Home tab of the Ribbon, click the dialog launcher in the Font group to bring up the Font dialog box, and choose All Caps.

If you are following the makeover step by step, continue using your saved presentation. If you just stepped in, you can use the `halloween_03.pptx` presentation from the `Makeover 05\Steps` folder on the CD.

For now, you'll see that some of the slide titles are bold, while others are not. To remedy that, follow these steps:

1. Click the View tab on the Ribbon, and click Slide Master to get to the Master Editing view (refer to Figure 6.4 earlier in this chapter).

2. Within the Slide Master, click the active Master thumbnail (the larger thumbnail) in the Slides pane.

3. Select the Slide Title placeholder.

4. Click the Home tab on the Ribbon, and within the Font group, click the Bold option.

5. View all the Slide Layouts within this Slide Master to make sure that all slide titles are bold. Don't worry about the color of the slide titles for now; we'll look at colors in the next step of this makeover.

6. Click the Slide Master tab of the Ribbon, and click the Close Master View button.

7. Save your presentation.

Step 5.   Create New Theme Colors

The next step in our makeover is to create a Halloween-inspired set of theme colors. PowerPoint includes several Theme Color sets that you can use, but it is more satisfying to choose the colors on your own.

As you create this custom set, you will learn the underlying structure of a Theme Color set in PowerPoint and what role each individual color plays in the larger picture.

There's a limit of just one custom Theme Color set that gets saved inside your presentation, so if you create many custom Theme Color sets, make sure you create newer presentations for them all unless you want to overwrite your other custom Theme Color sets.

If you are following the makeover step by step, continue using your saved presentation. If you just stepped in, you can use the **halloween_04.pptx** presentation from the Makeover 05\Steps folder on the CD.

Follow these steps to create your own set of theme colors:

1. Click the Design tab on the Ribbon, and click the Colors button to view the Theme Colors gallery (see Figure 6.11).

2. Choose the Create New Theme Colors option to bring up a dialog box of the same name, as shown in Figure 6.12.

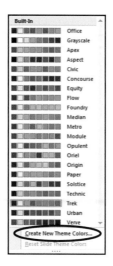

Figure 6.11

Your theme colors might be different than what is shown here.

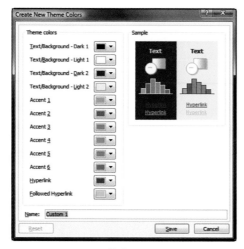

Before

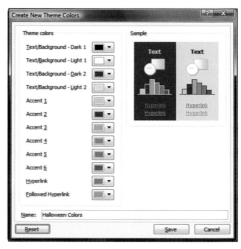

After

Figure 6.12

These dialog boxes show how the theme colors changed before and after I entered new color values.

Under the list of theme colors, you'll see 12 color swatches. These swatches represent the 12 colors that comprise a Theme Color set. In the remaining steps, I'll show you how you can change the colors within these swatches to create your own Theme Color set.

1. Toward the left of each swatch is an explanation of what that color signifies within a PowerPoint presentation; to learn more about these, refer to "The Twelve Theme Colors" section later in this chapter.

2. Click the down arrow next to each individual swatch, and you'll see a small color palette, as shown in Figure 6.13.

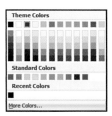

Figure 6.13

Click the More Colors option in the color palette.

3. Click the More Colors option to bring up the standard Windows color picker dialog box, which you can see in Figure 6.14.

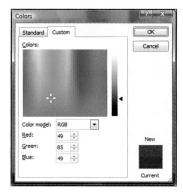

Figure 6.14

Enter the RGB color values provided in the table on this page.

4. Click the Custom tab in the dialog box, and enter the RGB values for each of the 12 swatches, as shown in Table 6.1. You won't have to change the Text/Background – Dark 1 and Text/Background – Light 1 colors, because they're the same as the original swatches.

Table 6.1 RGB Values for Custom Color Swatches

Swatch	RGB Value
Text/Background – Dark 1	R: 0 G: 0 B: 0
Text/Background – Light 1	R: 255 G: 255 B: 255
Text/Background – Dark 2	R: 49 G: 85 B: 49
Text/Background – Light 2	R: 213 G: 229 B: 209
Accent 1	R: 235 G: 230 B: 0
Accent 2	R: 37 G: 32 B: 249
Accent 3	R: 255 G: 162 B: 0
Accent 4	R: 118 G: 170 B: 36
Accent 5	R: 47 G: 149 B: 252
Accent 6	R: 219 G: 15 B: 23
Hyperlink	R: 237 G: 96 B: 46
Followed Hyperlink	R: 250 G: 142 B: 26

Click OK after you type in your color values for each individual swatch.

5. Name your Theme Color set in the Name text box (refer to Figure 6.12). Call it `Halloween Colors` or something similar, and then click the Save button to get back to your slide.

6. The new Theme Color set now is saved within your presentation. It also is applied to the presentation.

THE 12 THEME COLORS

So what do the 12 colors in a PowerPoint theme do? Where are they applied, and why should you even bother to create a Theme Color set? Wouldn't it be easier to choose any color that makes you happy?

These are valid questions, and I have equally valid answers for them!

First of all, you want your presentation slides to look consistent. You might be the only person creating slides, or you might be working in a company where many presentations are churned out each day, or you might be working in a large multinational organization where a presentation is being created this minute in some other part of the world. Whatever your situation, you want your slides to look coordinated, and deciding which theme colors you want to use in a presentation will save you a great deal of time in the future.

If you want to change the theme colors in all your slides or presentations, you can create a new Theme Colors set and apply it, so you are not really relegated to using the same colors—change is just a click away!

In the PowerPoint scheme of things, each of these 12 colors serves a purpose. More importantly, they need to relate to each other and coexist. For example, the background and text colors must be distinctly different to provide optimum contrast and readability.

Now that you have a better understanding of why it is important to choose these 12 colors, let me explain which part of the slide they influence:

Colors 1–4 are used for text and background. PowerPoint uses these names:

- Text/Background – Dark 1
- Text/Background – Light 1
- Text/Background – Dark 2
- Text/Background – Light 2

The first two colors normally are black and white, whereas the other two colors are dark and light variations of the same color, although you can use different colors as well. When PowerPoint has to decide which color to use as the default text color for a particular slide, it uses the rules shown in Table 6.2.

Table 6.2   Rules for Default Text Color

Background Color	Text Color
Dark 1	Light 1
Light 1	Dark 1
Dark 2	Light 2
Light 2	Dark 2

Colors 5–10 are the accent colors that are used as fills for shapes, diagrams, and charts that you create in PowerPoint. These accent colors are what determine the colors in the Quick Style galleries. Choosing these colors is not easy due to the following facts:

- The six colors have to look good on all four possible background choices.
- The colors must allow text in all four possible text colors to be contrasting and readable.
- They need to work well together.
- They also need to work well with colors 11 and 12, which we discuss next.

Colors 11 and 12 are used for two types of hyperlinks in the presentation:

- The Hyperlink color is used for linked content in a slide. The link might be to another slide, to another presentation or document, or even to a web address. Hyperlinked text shows up in PowerPoint with an underline.
- The Followed Hyperlink color is used for hyperlinks that already have been visited.

> **NOTE**
>
> Do you want viewers of the presentation to be unaware if a link already has been visited? If so, then use the same color for hyperlinks and visited hyperlinks!
>
> ---
>
> More often than not, you must carefully plan which colors work well together when you create a Theme Color set. If you are interested in working more with Theme Colors, some knowledge of color theory will help. Try looking at advertisements, websites, and presentations, and make a note of which colors work well together.
>
> The companion site for this book has some links to color resources:
>
> http://www.pptkit.com/color/
>
> Finally, it's important to understand that if you apply a different theme to a presentation, objects on the slides will take on the colors that are in the new Theme Color set.

Step 6.   Apply Theme Variations

The makeover is taking shape, but you probably can't help wondering when I am going to make the background and text colors look a little more appealing. Well, now is a good time to do that, so let me show you how you can change the backgrounds and text in a slide without changing the theme.

Each theme includes four background and text colors, as you learned in the preceding section. Figuring out which of these four colors work best is a trial-and-error process.

If you are following the makeover step by step, continue using your saved presentation. If you just stepped in, you can use the `halloween_05.pptx` presentation from the Makeover 05\Steps folder on the CD.

1. Click the Design tab on the Ribbon, and click the Background Styles button to view the gallery shown in Figure 6.15.

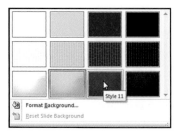

Figure 6.15

Change the background color, and PowerPoint changes the text color, too.

2. As you hover your cursor over the 12 background options in this gallery, you will see some changes preview in the active slide.

3. Each background style has a name that you can see as a ToolTip when you hover your cursor over its thumbnail in the Backgrounds gallery (refer to Figure 6.15). Choose the style named Style 11, and your text suddenly will be much more readable.

4. Save your presentation.

Step 7.   Add and Rename Slide Layouts

The ability to create Slide Layouts is a powerful new feature in PowerPoint 2007. PowerPoint comes with many types of Slide Layouts, including Title Slide Layouts, Title and Content Layouts, Section Header Layouts, and so on. You can even create your own layouts and name them anything you want!

Although our makeover presentation has several Picture Slide Layouts, it does not use them optimally. This step in the makeover shows you how to boost the visual interest of the presentation by improving the Picture Slide Layouts. You can apply these same techniques to create any type of Slide Layout.

TIP

This section shows you how you can create picture Slide Layouts, but what might be less obvious is that all Slide Layouts can be created the same way!

If you are following the makeover step by step, continue using your saved presentation. If you just stepped in, you can use the **halloween_06.pptx** presentation from the Makeover 05\Steps folder on the CD.

Follow these steps to create and edit your own picture Slide Layouts:

1. Click the View tab on the Ribbon, and click the Slide Master button to view the presentation in Slide Master view (refer to Figure 6.4 earlier in this chapter).

2. In the Slides pane on the left side of the screen, you'll find a set of slides identified by one large thumbnail (the Slide Master) and several smaller thumbnails (the Slide Layouts). If your presentation includes more than one Slide Master, you'll find several such Master and Layout sets.

3. Scroll down the Slides pane to see all the layouts. You'll find four picture Slide Layouts, which can be identified by the large, empty boxes that currently are empty picture placeholders. As you hover your cursor over any of them, you'll see that the ToolTip provides a name for the layout (see Figure 6.16).

Figure 6.16

Each layout has a name, as you can see in the ToolTip.

4. It is helpful to give the layouts more descriptive names. To do that, right-click on the Slide Layout that you want to rename, and choose Rename Layout, as shown in Figure 6.17.

5. This brings up the Rename Layout dialog box, as shown in Figure 6.18. Change the default name to a nice, descriptive name. I chose Large, Wide Picture with Caption, but you could choose anything else.

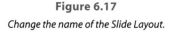

Figure 6.17

Change the name of the Slide Layout.

Figure 6.18

Provide a name you like.

6. Rename all the picture Slide Layouts (or even all the Slide Layouts) the same way.

TIP

You might wonder why you should bother with renaming a Slide Layout. You can actually opt not to rename a layout if you are creating a presentation that you never will use again. However, if you want to share this presentation with other users who will make changes to the presentation, or even if you might want to edit the same presentation after a few weeks or months, renaming a layout will help you understand the purpose you had for creating the new Slide Layout in the first place. In addition, maybe you'll end up becoming so good at designing Slide Layouts that you will make a business out of creating them!

7. Now it's time to create a new Slide Layout. Select the active Slide Master thumbnail in the Slides pane, and click the Insert Layout button on the Slide Master tab of the Ribbon.

You'll find a new Slide Layout thumbnail in the tree within the selected Slide Master, as you can see in Figure 6.19.

New Slide Layout

Figure 6.19

Adding a new Slide Layout.

8. Right-click this layout and choose Rename Layout (refer to Figure 6.18).

Give a name to the layout. For example, I just called it `My New Picture Layout 01`, but you could call it anything you want.

Adding Placeholders to the Slide Layout

Now you have a blank Slide Layout with a Title placeholder (and possibly a placeholder for the date and the footer). Delete the date and footer placeholders for now; you can do this by selecting the dashed placeholder outline and pressing the Delete key on your keyboard.

Now you are ready to insert new placeholders. To begin, follow these steps:

1. Insert one picture placeholder by clicking the Insert Placeholder button on the Slide Master tab of the Ribbon to open the Placeholder gallery that you can see in Figure 6.20. Choose the Picture option, and you'll be returned to your Slide Layout. Your mouse cursor will look like a crosshair.

2. Drag the cursor to create a picture placeholder, as shown in Figure 6.20.

Figure 6.20

Add a picture placeholder from the Placeholder gallery; then drag to create it on the slide.

TIP

You can insert more than one picture placeholder in a Slide Layout.

Resizing Picture Placeholders

Now you need to resize the picture placeholder. For most situations, you'll want to resize it to use one of these proportions:

- Height: 3 and Width: 4 for landscape-oriented pictures
- Height: 4 and Width: 3 for portrait-oriented pictures

NOTE

The reason to use these proportions is not difficult to discover; almost all digital cameras out there shoot using these proportions, and unless you have a good reason to use another proportion (perhaps your camera uses the conventional film proportion of 3:2, you have a new camera that has wide-angle shots of 16:9, or you just must have square shots!), you'll want to stick with these values.

---

1. To resize the picture placeholder, right-click it and choose the Size and Position option to bring up a dialog box of the same name, as shown in Figure 6.21.

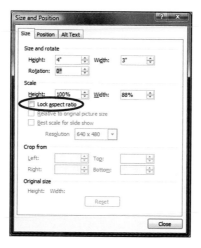

Figure 6.21

Resize the picture placeholder.

2. Within the Size tab of this dialog box, first make sure that the Lock Aspect Ratio check box is unchecked. Then, type in the size values in the Height and Width boxes.

   For a landscape-oriented picture, you could type **3** inches (height) by **4** inches (width). If you want to place just one larger picture in the Slide Layout, you could type **4.5** inches (height) and **6** inches (width), or you could type these in centimeters if your version of PowerPoint shows centimeters rather than inches. These are all 4 (width) × 3 (height) aspect ratios.

   For a portrait-oriented picture, you could type **4** inches (height) by **3** inches (width). If you want to place just one larger picture, you could type **6** inches (height) and **4.5** inches (width), or you could type these in centimeters if your version of PowerPoint shows centimeters rather than inches. These are all 3 (width) × 4 (height) aspect ratios.

3. After you have resized the placeholder, check the Lock Aspect Ratio check box to enable this option, and click Close.

4. If desired, add another picture placeholder in the same way, even on the same slide. Remember that you can add any combination of placeholders in the following list to build your picture Slide Layout:

   - Two landscape pictures

   - Two portrait pictures

   - One portrait picture and one landscape picture

   - One larger landscape picture

   - One larger portrait picture

5. Add a text placeholder on the slide if you want to use a caption for the pictures (remember that you already have a title placeholder). Including both a title *and* a text placeholder is completely optional. You'll have to make this decision based on your presentation's requirements. Inserting a text placeholder is easy; just use the instructions given for adding a picture placeholder and choose Text from the Placeholder gallery shown in Figure 6.20.

Final Adjustments to the Picture Slide Layout

Rearrange the position of the placeholders as needed. You can move the title below the pictures or drag the title a little to the right (see Figure 6.22). You can place picture placeholders close to each other or apart; you also can place the picture placeholders next to each other, but place one at a higher level than the other to create an interesting layout (again, see Figure 6.22). In addition, don't forget that you can slightly rotate your picture placeholders!

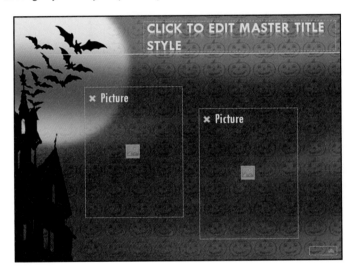

Figure 6.22
Experiment with the placements of the picture placeholders.

TIP

To rotate your placeholders, just select them; the placeholders then will be crowned with a green handle. Drag this handle to the left or right to rotate as required.

Click the Close Master View button on the Slide Master tab on the Ribbon to get back to your presentation. Save your presentation.

Step 8.   Refine Your Picture Placeholders

Picture placeholders don't have to be plain. In addition, if you don't want to go overboard with the effects, you still can apply some subtle changes to the placeholders so that the pictures you'll insert within the placeholders will look more elegant.

If you are following the makeover step by step, continue using your saved presentation. If you just stepped in, you can use the **halloween_07.pptx** presentation from the Makeover 05\Steps folder on the CD.

Follow these steps to fine-tune the placeholder settings:

1. Click the View tab on the Ribbon, and choose the Slide Master option. In the Slides pane, select the new Slide Layout that we created in the preceding section.

   If you did not follow the preceding section and instead opened the **halloween_07.pptx** presentation from the CD, the Slide Layout you want is the one at the bottom of the other layouts.

2. Select one or more picture placeholders on the Slide Layout. If you have more than one picture placeholder, you can select the first placeholder, then hold the Shift key and select the other placeholder, and repeat the steps for any more picture placeholders.

   Right-click the selected picture placeholders and choose Format Shape (or Format Object) to bring up the Format Shape dialog box (see Figure 6.23).

Figure 6.23
The default settings in the Format Shape dialog box.

3. Click Fill on the left, and opt for a Solid fill. Click the Color button to view the Theme Colors, and select the black swatch at the top left.

4. Next, click Line Color on the left, and choose the Solid line color. Click the Color button to view the theme colors, and select the Accent 1 color (yellow in this theme). See Figure 6.24.

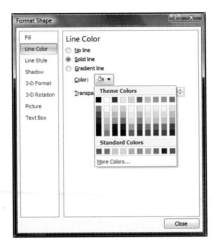

Figure 6.24
Select a line color.

5. Click the Close button to get back to your slide layout.

6. Next, let's add some reflection to the picture placeholders. To do that, select one or more of the picture placeholders. Then, click the Drawing Tools Format tab on the Ribbon. Click the Shape Effects option to view the Effects gallery shown in Figure 6.25.

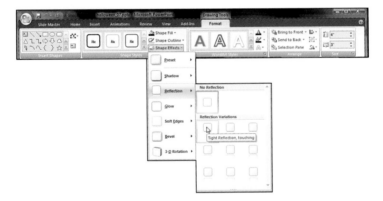

Figure 6.25
The Effects gallery lets you add sophisticated effects with one click.

TIP

If you can't see the Drawing Tools Format tab, or any of the other context-sensitive tabs on the Ribbon, you might not have selected a slide object.

Many of these tabs are activated only if you select a corresponding object. Thus, if you select a shape on the slide, you should be seeing the Drawing Tools Format tab on the Ribbon.

---

7. Choose the Reflection option to view the Reflection subgallery (refer to Figure 6.25). Within the Reflection subgallery, explore the options in the Reflection Variations section. I chose the top-left option to provide a very subtle reflection effect.

8. Click the Slide Master tab on the Ribbon, and click the Close Master View option to get back to the default PowerPoint interface. Save your presentation.

Step 9.   Apply Slide Layouts

After you create and fine-tune the picture Slide Layouts as explained in the preceding sections, you need to apply those layouts to the picture slides.

If you are following the makeover step by step, continue using your saved presentation. If you just stepped in, you can use the **halloween_08.pptx** presentation from the Makeover 05\Steps folder on the CD.

Follow these steps to apply the picture Slide Layout to slides in your presentation:

1. Make sure that the visible slide in Normal view is the one for which you want to change the Slide Layout. For now, I am choosing slide 3 (see Figure 6.26) because it has two tall pictures like the new Slide Layout we created in the preceding steps.

TIP

When you apply a new Slide Layout from the Layout gallery (refer to Figure 6.27), it is applied by default to the active slide. That should be fine in this case, but if you want to apply the same Slide Layout to multiple slides, you need to select all the slides that you want to change within Slide Sorter view. Then follow the rest of the steps in this step sequence.

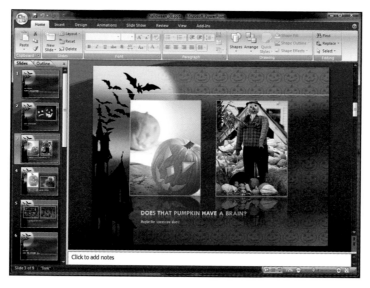

Figure 6.26

This is how the slide looks in its existing layout.

2. Click the Home tab on the Ribbon, and then click the Layout option to open the Layout Gallery shown in Figure 6.27. Note that the new picture Slide Layout that you created now shows up within this drop-down gallery (see the last layout in Figure 6.27).

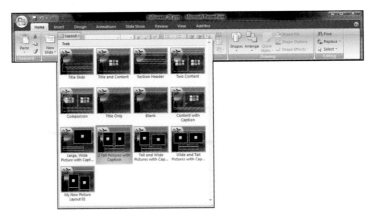

Figure 6.27
The layouts you create can be the layouts you apply!

CAUTION

If the new Slide Layout doesn't show up in the Layout gallery, that means you haven't created any new Slide Layouts. Or maybe you are working with the wrong presentation!

3. Click the picture Slide Layout in the Layout gallery that you want to apply to the selected slide (or slides). If you don't like the layout you chose, or if you clicked the wrong layout, press Ctrl+Z to undo the last step.

4. Sometimes, applying a Slide Layout alters the orientation of pictures already inserted in the slides. For example, a landscape-oriented picture might show up in your portrait-oriented picture placeholder. To correct this, simply resize the placeholders, or change the pictures within the placeholders to ones that fit the placeholder on the slide itself.

TIP

You can change the picture in a placeholder by using the Change Picture option in the Picture Tools Format tab on the Ribbon. This tab normally is not visible—it shows up only when you select the picture or picture placeholder on the slide. Or you can always just right-click the picture or picture placeholder and choose Change Picture.

5. Continue following steps 1–4 until you have finished applying new Slide Layouts to all the slides you want to update. Tweak the placeholders if the picture orientations change, as explained in step 4.

Remember to save your PowerPoint presentation often as you continue to make changes!

Step 10. Slide Layout Finishing Touches

Although adding a new Slide Layout is easy, editing existing layouts is simpler than creating them again from scratch.

We did create a new picture Slide Layout, but our makeover presentation already contains several other picture Slide Layouts, as you might remember from our short renaming spree earlier in this chapter. While most of these Slide Layouts look similar to the new Slide Layout we created, you'll find that the placement of slide titles is not consistent on all the layouts. In addition, the font size of the titles in some of these is different.

If you are following the makeover step by step, continue using your saved presentation. If you just stepped in, you can use the **halloween_09.pptx** presentation from the Makeover 05\Steps folder on the CD.

Follow these steps to create consistent-looking slide titles:

1. View the Slide Master of the presentation by clicking the View tab on the Ribbon and clicking the Slide Master button.

2. Select any one of the picture Slide Layouts in the Slides pane. Most of the time, you will have trouble selecting the objects on the Slide Layout itself, including some title placeholders, because the reflection effects added to the picture placeholders earlier in this makeover might be placed over the titles as well. This isn't always noticeable because most of the reflections are quite transparent.

    To rectify this, select each of the picture placeholders, right-click, and click the Send to Back option in the resulting context menu. Do this on all Slide Layouts that contain picture place-holders.

3. Next, select the new picture Slide Layout that you created earlier in this makeover. Click the Title placeholder. Select all the text within the title and right-click to access the mini toolbar shown in Figure 6.28. As you can see in the figure, the font size is 32.

    Select the title placeholders in all the other picture Slide Layouts, and change their font sizes to 32 as well. Don't worry if some of the title placeholders look out of place; we'll fix that soon.

4. Remove the footer, slide number, and date placeholders from all the picture Slide Layouts, if you want. It's not necessary to remove these unless you like to have them out of the way. To do this, make sure that the Slide Master tab on the Ribbon is active, and uncheck the Footers option.

Figure 6.28

Change the font size of the title placeholders.

5. Resize and reposition all the title placeholders as required. You might want to give them a larger area for the increased font size. Whatever you do, make sure that all the title placeholders are sized and positioned consistently across all the Slide Layouts. That's easy to do if you note the size and position values found on the Size tab of the Size and Position dialog box. Access this box by selecting the placeholder, right-clicking, and choosing the Size and Position option (see Figure 6.29).

Figure 6.29

Make a note of your new Size and Position coordinates.

6. After you clean up the title placeholders, you might want to reposition other elements as well. For example, you might want to reposition the text boxes for subtitles or captions, change their font sizes, and add reflections to text. Why would you want to add reflections to text? Because it looks *trés* cool!

7. Remember that you can add the effect to all titles or placeholders in a presentation by formatting the appropriate placeholder in the Slide Master.

   As soon as you select the title placeholder, a new tab called Drawing Tools Format is visible on the Ribbon. Click this tab.

8. In the WordArt Styles group, click the down arrow next to the Text Effects button to open a gallery. Select the Reflection option to open a subgallery (as shown in Figure 6.30).

Figure 6.30
Add reflected text.

9. You can choose from any of the reflection options. For the purposes of our makeover, choose the top-middle option called Half Reflection, Touching.

10. If you are in Slide Master view, click the View tab on the Ribbon, and click Normal. Remember to save your presentation.

I also chose to change the font sizes for the subtitles for our makeover presentation. Open the `halloween_10.pptx` (the next file in this makeover sequence) presentation from the `Makeover 05\Steps` folder on the CD to see the result.

Step 11.   Create or Import Graphic Elements

In the same way that you might put some embellishments on a paper scrapbook, you can add graphic elements in PowerPoint.

There are many ways you can do this:

- Draw a shape or a line. Add effects and color fills to shapes or lines and place them over the pictures, or just slightly overlap the edges of the pictures.

- Create your own simple graphics using another program, such as Windows Paint. You also can use a more advanced program such as Adobe Photoshop to create graphics for your layout and save them as PNGs with transparent backdrops. Place those PNGs on the slide wherever required. Duplicate the same PNG several times, and then add variation to the duplicated PNGs by resizing and rotating them differently.

- Insert small graphics. Choose small pictures with transparent backgrounds from PowerPoint's Clip Art task pane.

- Add small text notes. Add text such as "Wow," "Awesome," "Happiness," and so on, and then format them with WordArt styles.

Whatever you do, make sure that the end results are more subtle than dramatic. In addition, remember that you can add these graphic elements to individual layouts in the Slide Master as well.

GRADIENT LINES

Look at the lines you can see in Figure 6.31. These thick lines are colored with more than one color. New for PowerPoint 2007, these gradient lines can blend many, many colors to create a unique statement. However, be careful with the colors—just because you can create a line that contains six colors is no reason to use them all!

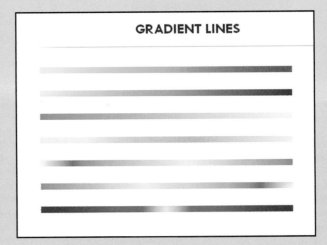

Figure 6.31

Lines in rainbow colors.

Try creating gradient lines that use monochromatic colors, such as six shades of the blue-gray family starting from a vivid turquoise to the palest gray.

To apply a gradient to a line, remember that you need a somewhat-thick line to show off all the colors. A one-point line hardly will benefit from six colors. As a rule of thumb, a 15-point line is a good starting point, although sometimes you can go as low as 10 points.

To apply a gradient to a line, follow these steps:

1. Draw a line, or select an existing line. The line does not even have to be a conventional, straight line; it also can be the outline of a selected rectangle or another shape. Either way, the important part is that it should be selected.

2. Right-click the selected line or shape to access the context menu. Choose the Format Shape option to bring up a dialog box of the same name.

3. Click Line Color on the left of this dialog box, as shown in Figure 6.32, and then click the Gradient Lines option to alter the options available.

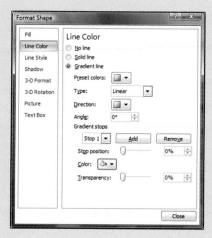

Figure 6.32
Line Color is where you'll find all the gradient line options.

4. Choose a preset gradient option, or play with the gradient settings. Choosing a preset option does free you from creating your own gradient, but a little time spent in working with the other options will go a long way in helping you create more coordinated gradients. Figure 6.33 shows you a selection of preset gradient styles that are available.

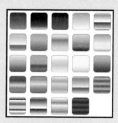

Figure 6.33
Use these preset gradients as a starting point to create new gradients.

Now let's add some ornamental elements to make your pictures stand out even more. Because this is a Halloween presentation, I selected the bat, as shown in Figure 6.34, to add some creepiness to the slides!

Figure 6.34

Unleash this bat on your slides.

You'll find this bat picture (**bat3.png**) in the `Makeover 05\Steps` folder on the CD. If you are following the makeover step by step, continue using your saved presentation. If you just stepped in, you can use the **halloween_10.pptx** presentation from the `Makeover 05\Steps` folder on the CD.

Follow these steps to bring in the bats:

1. View the Slide Master of the presentation by clicking the View tab on the Ribbon and clicking the Slide Master button.

2. Select any of the picture Slide Layouts, and then click the Insert tab on the Ribbon. Click the Picture button to bring up the Insert Picture dialog box. Navigate to wherever you saved the bat image (or go straight to the `Makeover 05\Pictures` folder on the CD), and select the **bat3.png** file. Click the Insert button to get back to your Slide Layout.

3. As you can see in Figure 6.35, the bat seems to be enjoying the attention it can get by sitting over the two picture placeholders. Cut him down to size by clicking and dragging one of the corner handles on the bounding box toward the center of the box. Now you can click and drag the bat and place him anywhere you fancy. If you want two bats, just duplicate the existing one by right-clicking it and choosing Copy, and then right-clicking again and choosing Paste. Click and drag it to place it elsewhere on the slide. The second slide in Figure 6.35 shows how interesting this can look.

4. Using steps 2 and 3, add more bats to the other Slide Layouts in the presentation. In some of the Slide Layouts, you can rotate the bats as you like. After the bat is selected, drag the top green handle as required to rotate it.

5. Click the Slide Master tab on the Ribbon, and click the Close Master View button to get back to your slides. Save your presentation.

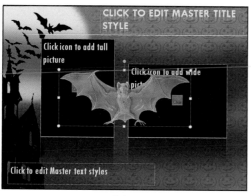
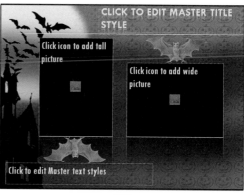

Before   After

Figure 6.35
How much difference can those bats make?

WHY ARE THE BATS TRANSPARENT?

Well, the bats are not actually transparent, but they are on a transparent background. Thus, you don't end up with a white or black box showing behind them when you place them on your slide. They can sit wherever they want, and the background of the slide shows through around them.

This happens because the bat picture you inserted was a PNG file with transparency. Of all the picture file formats, only a few can support transparency; they are PNG, TIFF, and GIF. While PNG and TIFF files can support varying levels of transparency, GIFs can support only a single level of transparency—this means some areas are either transparent or not. PNGs and TIFFs, on the other hand, support semi-transparent areas as well.

These PNGs and TIFFs need to be created in a specialized application such as Adobe Photoshop or something similar.

Step 12.   Add Scary Music

There's one last flourish you can add to the presentation to really add to the Halloween atmosphere: a scary music track.

If you are following the makeover step by step, continue using your saved presentation. If you just stepped in, you can use the `halloween_11.pptx` presentation from the `Makeover 05` folder on the CD.

Here's how you can add some scary music:

1. Because we are going to insert a sound clip from Microsoft's Office Online collection, we need to be sure that the sound inserted is embedded within the presentation file itself, just in case you need to copy the presentation to another computer and discover that the sound no longer plays.

   To do that, choose Office Button, PowerPoint Options to bring up a dialog box of the same name. Click Advanced on the left, and scroll down a little on the right side under Save so that you can set the Link Sounds Larger Than parameter. Change that to 1000 kb, as shown in Figure 6.36. Click OK to get back to your presentation.

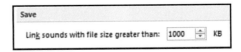

Figure 6.36

Set the sound file size parameter.

2. Make sure you are on the first slide of the presentation. Now click the Insert tab on the Ribbon, and click the small arrow below the Sound button to bring up the short list that you can see in Figure 6.37.

Figure 6.37

Bring in the sounds.

3. Choose the Sound from Clip Organizer option to activate the Clip Art task pane that you see in Figure 6.38. At this point, if PowerPoint asks you for permission to search Microsoft's online media collection, say yes.

Figure 6.38

A library of sounds.

4. Type **scary** in the Search For text box, and click the Go button. Assuming you are connected online, PowerPoint will search Microsoft's media servers for scary sounds and show you the results within the pane (refer to Figure 6.38).

TIP

If you choose to insert sound by clicking the Clip Art button on the Insert tab of the Ribbon, you will need to click the Results Should Be option in the Clip Art pane and choose Sound to filter the search to just sound files. This is one reason it's easier just to choose the Sound button on the Insert tab of the Ribbon.

5. You can preview any of the sounds by right-clicking the sound icon in the pane and choosing the Preview/Properties dialog box, as shown in Figure 6.39.

6. To insert the sound, right-click the sound icon in the pane, and choose Insert. We chose a clip called Horror Full Mix. PowerPoint will show you a dialog box that lets you decide whether you want the sound to start automatically or when clicked. Choose the Automatically option.

7. You'll see a sound icon right in the middle of your slide. In addition, the Ribbon will show you the Sound Tools Options tab, as shown in Figure 6.390. In the Play Sound drop-down list, choose the Play Across Slides option, and check the Loop Until Stopped check box.

Figure 6.39

Play that eerie sound across all slides.

8. You now can drag that sound icon off the slide area to get it out of view.

9. Save your presentation.

You can view (and hear) the finished presentation, **halloween_12.pptx** from the Makeover 05\Steps folder on the CD.

Before

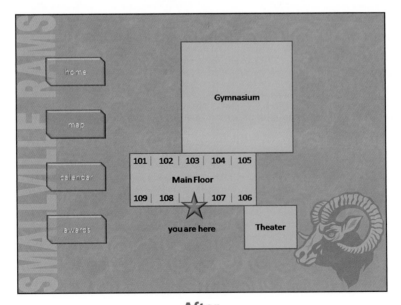

After

ON THE CD:

The sample presentation and all other files with which you need to work can be found on the CD in the `Makeover 06` folder.

7

Makeover 6: Kiosk Presentation

YOU WILL LEARN HOW TO:

- Modify Slide Layouts
- Work in Slide Master View
- Kern Text
- Add Text Effects
- Create Hyperlinks
- Use Trigger Animations
- Use Kiosk Mode
- Work with Shapes

About This Makeover

This presentation runs on an unattended computer in the entryway of the local high school. It's set up so that each slide advances to the next automatically after five seconds, and the entire presentation runs in a continuous loop. Because there are eight slides, the entire presentation takes about 40 seconds to cycle.

To make this presentation easier for the user to quickly get to the information he really wants to see, we'll use PowerPoint's Browsed at a kiosk show type, which allows users to click buttons to navigate from slide to slide in any order they choose. And, of course, we'll create those buttons, too. We'll also make the presentation look better in the process!

Our kiosk presentation will have a Home slide, a slide showing a clickable map of the school, another slide with a calendar of events, and a slide listing awards various clubs or teams have received.

Step 1.   Create and Apply Appropriate Slide Layouts

Open the original presentation, `kiosk_00.pptx`, by selecting Office Button, Open. This file can be found on the CD in the `Makeover 06\Steps` folder.

The ram mascot logos on the four corners of the slide do not provide a sophisticated look (see Figure 7.1). Replacing these four logos with just one larger variation of the logo in the lower-right corner of the slide will allow the ram's head to look onto the slide instead of away from it. This position, along with the added transparency (see Figure 7.2), help the logo blend in to the background better, allowing for a more cohesive and understated look. It also gives more room without distracting from the content of the slides.

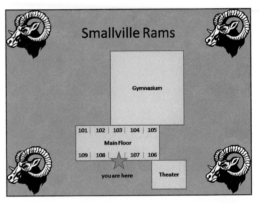

Figure 7.1
Clean and functional, but certainly not contemporary.

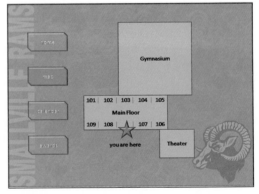

Figure 7.2
Notice that the ram is now larger and semi-transparent.

Reposition and Fade the Logo

To add and position a new logo, follow these steps:

1. Open the **kiosk_00.pptx** presentation from the Makeover 06\Steps folder on the CD. Select the View tab on the Ribbon, and then click Slide Master to open Slide Master View, as shown in Figure 7.3.

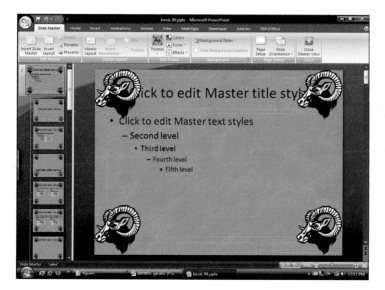

Figure 7.3

The slides pane on the left contains the Slide Master and layouts.

2. In the slides pane, click the Slide Master, the larger thumbnail at the top (refer to Figure 7.3).

3. Select the four ram head images, and press the Delete key to remove them.

4. Scroll down the layouts in the slides pane, and select the Blank layout. You'll be able to identify the Blank layout because it has almost no placeholders, and you'll also see a ToolTip called Blank Layout.

5. Now we'll insert a new semitransparent logo on the Blank layout. Select the Insert tab of the Ribbon, and then click Picture. This brings up the Insert Picture dialog box. Navigate to the Makeover 06\Steps folder on the CD and choose the **light_ramshead.emf** picture, and then click Insert at the bottom of the dialog box to return to the Slide Master.

6. Click the Picture Tools Format tab on the Ribbon. In the Size group, type **5.25** in the Shape Height box (see Figure 7.4). When you click away from the Shape Height box or press Enter, the logo will resize proportionately.

Figure 7.4

Type the height and width of your image here.

7. Drag the logo to the bottom-right corner of the slide.

MAKING CLIP ART TRANSPARENT

You can make the existing logos on the slide background transparent by following these steps:

1. Insert the `ram.emf` clip art from the `Makeover 06\Pictures` folder on the CD onto your slide background. Select the logo and choose the Picture Tools Format tab on the Ribbon; then in the Arrange group, choose Group, Ungroup.

2. PowerPoint will ask you whether you want to convert the picture into a Microsoft Office Drawing Object. Click Yes.

3. Choose the Drawing Tools Format tab on the Ribbon; then in the Arrange group, choose Group, Ungroup.

4. The clip art will be ungrouped into its individual pieces. Click anywhere on the slide to deselect all the clip objects.

5. Select any individual piece and change its color or transparency by clicking the Drawing Tools Format tab on the Ribbon; then in the Shape Styles group, choose Shape Fill, More Fill Colors. Next, move the transparency slider toward 100% to make the selected object more transparent.

6. Sometimes when clips are ungrouped, there is more than one layer of individual objects. If you are having trouble setting transparency on an object, be sure there's not an identical object lurking behind it! The Selection and Visibility pane on the Home tab of the Ribbon can help with this. Also, when you ungroup clip art, an empty bounding box almost always appears on top of the ungrouped elements. You'll want to delete it because it's just an extra blank object you don't need.

7. Regroup the clip by selecting one of the pieces and choosing the Drawing Tools Format tab on the Ribbon; then in the Arrange group, choose Group, then Regroup. You also can select all the pieces and click the Drawing Tools Format tab on the Ribbon; then in the Arrange group, choose Group, then Group. This often gives you a closer frame area for the clip, especially if you deleted the empty bounding box as mentioned in step 6.

8. Delete this logo before proceeding with the chapter.

Making clips transparent can be tedious; that's why we did it for you!

Create Graphic Text

Having the school mascot name look like typical text in a regular presentation is boring, so let's give the text some oomph and make it look more like a graphic.

To add graphic elements to text, follow these steps:

1. You are still in Slide Master view in the Blank layout, as explained in the preceding steps. Now choose the Home tab on the Ribbon, then Shapes, then Text Box (the first shape in the Basic Shapes section). Click on the slide and type SMALLVILLE RAMS.

2. Select all the text, right-click, and choose Arial Black on the mini toolbar that pops up. Change the font size to 48 point using the font size drop-down. Click the arrow next to the Font Color icon and choose More Colors. On the Custom tab, type RGB values 92, 172, 238 (see Figure 7.5). Click OK to close the dialog box.

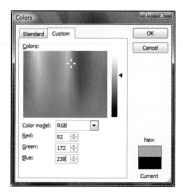

Figure 7.5

You can always specify Red, Green, and Blue color values in the Colors dialog box on the Custom tab.

3. Rotate the text box 90 degrees counterclockwise by choosing the Home tab on the Ribbon. Then in the Drawing group click the Arrange button, and choose Rotate, Rotate Left 90°. Drag the end of the text box to fill the height of the slide (see Figure 7.6).

4. Right-click the text box and choose Format Shape. In the Format Shape dialog box, choose Text Box in the list on the left. Set all four internal margins to 0". Click Close to close the dialog box.

5. To make the text fill the text box, choose the Drawing Tools Format tab on the Ribbon; then in the Word Art Styles group, click the Text Effects button to display a drop-down gallery. Click Transform, and in the Transform gallery, choose Warp, Square (see Figure 7.7).

Figure 7.6

Drag any of the white handles to resize the text box.

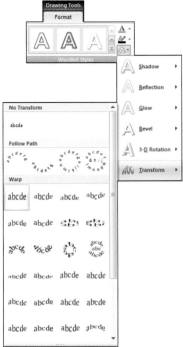

Figure 7.7

Use Transform text effects to reshape text.

6. Drag the text box handle next to the green rotation circle until the text box is as wide as you want, about 1.25".

7. Select the "E" in SMALLVILLE and the "R" in RAMS. Choose the Home tab on the Ribbon; then in the Font group, click the Character Spacing button to display a short list. Choose More Spacing to open a dialog box. Specify Expanded by 3.8 pt to increase the space between the two words. Feel free to adjust the spacing on other letter pairs. For example, we also specified "condensed by 2 pts" for the adjacent "L" and "V" in SMALLVILLE. Look at Figure 7.8 to see the result.

TIP

Before performing step 7, you might need to go to the Office Button and select PowerPoint Options. Then click Advanced and uncheck When Selecting, Automatically Select Entire Word.

Figure 7.8
Changing the logo and text gives this slide a much more sophisticated feel.

Duplicate and Reorder the Layouts

This layout will work beautifully for our Home slide, but we should make another layout with a little smaller logo for the rest of the slides. We should also delete all these extraneous layouts, because there's really no reason to keep them.

To create a duplicate layout with a smaller logo, do the following:

1. Still in Slide Master View, right-click the Blank Layout in the slides pane and choose Rename Layout. Type **Home** in the Layout Name box and click Rename.

2. Right-click Home Layout and choose Duplicate layout.

3. Select the duplicated layout and choose Rename Layout. Type **Body** in the Layout name box and click Rename.

4. Select the Body Layout in the slides pane, and on the slide, select the logo. Click Picture Tools Format on the Ribbon; then in the Size group, type **2.7** in the Shape Height box. When you click away from the Shape Height box or press Enter, the logo will resize proportionately. Drag the logo to the lower-right corner of the slide.

5. Delete the other slide layouts by selecting them in the slides pane and pressing Delete on your keyboard. You will not be able to delete some of the layouts because slides in the presentation are based on those layouts. It's not a problem, so just delete what you can. Don't delete the Title Slide layout or your file won't have a Windows preview image.

6. Choose the View tab on the Ribbon, and then choose Normal to close Slide Master View.

Apply Slide Layouts

To apply slide layouts, follow these steps:

1. In Normal editing view, select the first slide in the slides pane.

2. Choose the Home tab on the Ribbon; then click Layout to open the Layout gallery and choose Home.

3. Select slides 2 and 3 in the slides pane by Ctrl+clicking them; choose the Home tab on the Ribbon, and then choose Body in the Layout gallery.

4. Add a new slide 4 by selecting slide 3 and choosing the Home tab on the Ribbon; then choose New Slide. A new slide with the Body layout will be created.

TIP

If you click the top of the New Slide button, a new slide is automatically inserted, and it uses the layout of the slide you have selected in the slide pane. Clicking the bottom of the New Slide button opens the layout gallery so you can choose which layout you want.

---

5. Delete the text boxes with Smallville Rams from slides 1, 2, and 3.

6. Save your presentation.

Now that our main slides look better, we're ready to create the navigation!

Step 2.   Create Buttons and Add Links for Navigation

We've really condensed our kiosk presentation to four slides: the Home slide, a map slide, a calendar slide, and a fourth slide, which will be used for awards. Now we have to make it easy for users to navigate to those slides.

If you are following the makeover step by step, just continue using your saved presentation. If you just stepped in, you can use the **kiosk_01.pptx** presentation from the Makeover 06\Steps folder on the CD.

Create the Buttons

To create shapes to use as buttons, do the following:

1. On Slide 1, choose the Home tab on the Ribbon, then in the Drawing group, click the Shapes button to open the Shapes gallery. In the Rectangles section of the Shapes gallery, click the Snip Diagonal Corner Rectangle. Click the slide to create a shape.

2. When the shape is selected on the slide, the Drawing Tools Format tab will be available in the Ribbon. Click it, and then type **.75** in the Shape Height box and **1.6** in the Shape Width box. The shape will be filled with the blue Accent 1 color automatically.

3. On the Drawing Tools Format tab on the Ribbon, choose Shape Fill, then More Fill Colors, and move the Transparency slider to 55%.

TIP

Making buttons semitransparent allows us to place them on top of the graphical text on the slide background without compromising readability.

---

4. Click Shape Effects, then Bevel, and then Circle (see Figure 7.9).

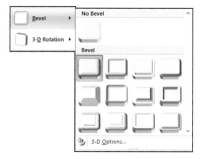

Figure 7.9

Bevels make shapes look more like buttons.

5. Select the button and type the word **home**.

6. Select the button, and then press Ctrl+Shift and drag downward to create a copy of the button. (Pressing Shift constrains the copy to the same horizontal or vertical edge as the original object.)

7. Type **map** in the new shape.

8. Repeat steps 6 and 7 to create two more buttons. Type **calendar** and **awards** in those buttons.

9. Select all four buttons by Shift+clicking each of them. Then, on the Home tab on the Ribbon, choose Arrange, then Align, and then Distribute Vertically to create equal distance between all the buttons.

Add Navigation Links

To add links to the buttons, do the following:

1. Select the map button. Choose the Insert tab on the Ribbon, and then click Hyperlink. Click the Bookmark button on the right side of the Insert Hyperlink dialog box. This opens the Select Place in Document dialog box (see Figure 7.10).

Figure 7.10
Clicking the Bookmark button on the Insert Hyperlink dialog box opens a dialog box with a list of slides in the presentation.

2. The map slide is slide 2, so select Slide 2 in the list and click OK to close the Select Place in Document dialog box. Click OK again to close the Insert Hyperlink dialog box.

TIP

The text in the Insert Hyperlink, Bookmark dialog box comes from the text in the title place-holder on the slide. If there is no title placeholder, the slides will be listed as Slide 1, Slide 2, and so on (refer to Figure 7.10). If you prefer to see slide titles here, but don't want the slide title to show on the slide, choose the Title Only slide layout and use the Selection and Visibility pane to make the title placeholder invisible.

---

3. Select the calendar button. Add a hyperlink to this button using steps 1 and 2. Choose Slide 3 from the list to go to the calendar slide.

4. Select the awards button. Add a hyperlink to this button using steps 1 and 2. Choose Slide 4 from the list to go to the awards slide.

5. Select the home button. Add a hyperlink to this button using steps 1 and 2. Choose Slide 1 from the list to go to the home slide of the kiosk.

Copy and Format the Buttons for Each Slide

We could add these buttons to the slide master or slide layouts, but it would be nice to highlight the appropriate button to help the user know which slide he's looking at. Because of this, we'll copy the buttons to each slide in our presentation. Simply select the four buttons, copy them (Ctrl+C), and paste them (Ctrl+V) on slides 2, 3, and 4.

To highlight one button on each slide, let's remove the transparency. This will make the button look darker.

1. On Slide 1, select the home button.

2. Select the Drawing Tools Format tab on the Ribbon; then click the Shape Fill button and choose More Fill Colors. Move the Transparency slider to 0% and click OK to close the dialog box.

3. Repeat for the map button on Slide 2, the calendar button on Slide 3, and the awards button on Slide 4 (see Figure 7.11).

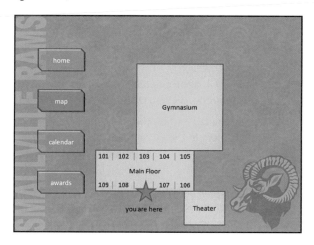

Figure 7.11

The darker buttons might not look as dark in print, but they look different on a screen. They are a subtle reminder of which slide you're looking at.

Step 3.   Improve the Appearance of Other Elements

If you are following the makeover step by step, just continue using your saved presentation. If you just stepped in, you can use the **kiosk_02.pptx** presentation from the Makeover 06\Steps folder on the CD.

Apply Transparency and Shape Effects

The Smallville Rams' school colors are faded blue and old gold. The map on slide 2 is a bit bright, but we can make it easier on the eyes by adding transparency. To do this, we selected the three yellow rectangles (Ctrl+click); then on the Drawing Tools Format tab on the Ribbon, we chose Shape Fill and then More Fill Colors, and then dragged the Transparency slider to 26%.

We also added some depth to the star to make this "you are here" indicator more visible. We selected the star, and back on the Drawing Tools Format tab, we chose Shape Styles, Shape Effects, Bevel, and finally, Circle. We also selected all the map items and dragged them higher on the slide.

Format the Calendar Table

The calendar table on slide 3 had a lot of formatting. Here's a list of what we did:

1. Resized the table to about 5.5"×6.1". After the table is selected, you can see this setting on the Table Tools Layout tab on the Ribbon in the Table Size group.

2. Selected all the text (and numbers) in the table, right-clicked, and changed the size to 20-point font using the font size drop-down on the mini toolbar. Set February to 36-point font.

3. Deleted the words "basketball game" from the 5th, 13th, and 27th squares and the words "South Pacific" from the 10th square.

4. Sized and distributed the table cells appropriately by choosing the Table Tools Layout tab on the Ribbon, and in the Cell Size group, clicking Distribute Rows and then Distribute Columns.

5. Added a fill color to all cells in the table using the Table Tools Design tab on the Ribbon, Table Styles, Shading, and More Fill Colors. In the Custom tab, we specified RGB values of 121, 181, and 218, and also selected 67% transparency. This helps "pop" the table off the slide while still allowing the ram mascot to show.

6. Inserted clip art to indicate basketball games on the 5th, 13th, and 27th. Chose the Insert tab on the Ribbon, then Clip Art, and then typed `basketball` into the Search For box (see Figure 7.12). Repeated the process using the word `theater` to search for and insert clip art indicating a play on the 10th.

7. We recolored the theater clip art by selecting the Picture Tools Format tab on the Ribbon; then in the Adjust group, we chose Recolor and Accent color 6 Dark. We also ungrouped the basketball clip art (refer to the "Making Clip Art Transparent" sidebar earlier in this chapter) and removed the motion lines. Of course, we made these clips smaller by dragging a corner handle, made copies of the basketball clip, and dragged them all into place on top of the table (compare Figure 7.13 to Figure 7.14). Leaving the clips a little brighter instead of changing them to a faded blue color helps them stand out against the calendar background.

Figure 7.12

Select the Insert tab on the Ribbon, and then click Clip Art to search for clip art and photographs on Microsoft Office Online.

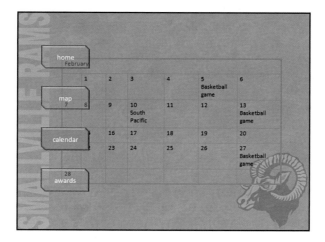

Figure 7.13

Here's what our original calendar looked like.

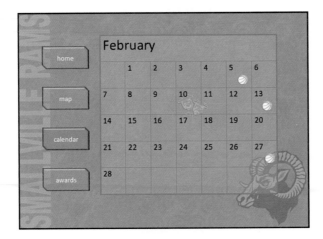

Figure 7.14

The revised calendar. It's amazing the difference a few changes can make!

8. As the final step, rename the clips. Click the Home tab on the Ribbon, and then in the Editing group, click Select, Selection Pane. Click the minus symbols to collapse the groups. Click a group name in the Selection and Visibility pane, and click again to rename it. When you select an object in the pane, it will be selected on the slide, and vice versa (see Figure 7.15). Naming the clips now will make it easier to apply animations later.

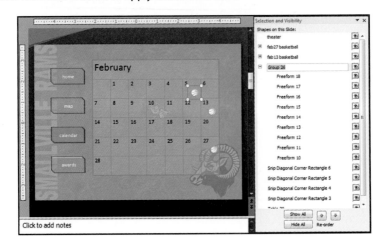

Figure 7.15

You can name objects on a slide in the Selection and Visibility pane.

Step 4.   Apply Trigger Animations

It would be really cool if people could click the clip art to get more information about the events listed on the calendar. We can use a trigger animation to show the information directly on the slide.

If you are following the makeover step by step, just continue using your saved presentation. If you just stepped in, you can use the `kiosk_03.pptx` presentation from the `Makeover 06\Steps` folder on the CD.

TIP

A hyperlink or action setting takes you to a different slide. A trigger animation animates an object on the same slide.

Add Shapes to Animate

To begin, first add the information about the February 5 basketball game to the slide following these steps:

1. Make sure you are on slide 3, and select the Home tab on the Ribbon; then in Drawing group, click the Shapes button. In the Shapes gallery, choose Snip Diagonal Corner Rectangle. Click the slide to add the shape.

2. Type the information from slide 6 into the shape. Drag one of the square white sizing handles to resize the shape. Drag and position the shape a little above the February 5 event on the table.

3. Rename the shape in the Selection and Visibility pane. We used `feb5 info`.

Apply Animations and Add Trigger Settings

To add an entrance animation effect, do the following:

1. Select the shape with the information about the February 5 game and choose the Animations tab on the Ribbon; then choose Animations, Custom Animation.

2. In the Custom Animation pane, click the Add Effect button, and then choose Entrance, Appear. If Appear doesn't show up on the list, choose More Effects (see Figure 7.16).

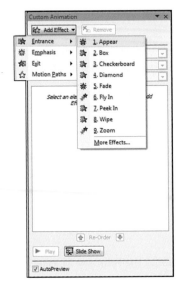

Figure 7.16

You can choose from four basic types of animations: entrance, emphasis, exit, and motion paths.

TIP

PowerPoint 2007's new small caps feature is the perfect thing to use when you see the "am" and "pm" text (indicating morning and evening, respectively) following time elements. Select the text and choose the Home tab on the Ribbon, click the Font group dialog launcher, and check the Small Caps option in the dialog box. You can see these small caps in the shapes on Figure 7.16.

---

3. In the Custom Animation pane, click the down arrow next to the animation effect and choose Timing (see Figure 7.17). This opens the Appear dialog box (the dialog box is named after the animation style used).

4. On the Timing tab in the Appear dialog box, click the Triggers button, and then choose Start Effect on Click Of. In the drop-down box, select the item you want to click to start the animation (see Figure 7.18). We've chosen feb5 basketball; now when we click the basketball on the February 5 square of the calendar, the information shape will appear.

Figure 7.17

Click the arrow next to the animation in the Custom Animation pane to get more options.

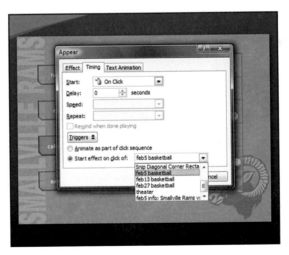

Figure 7.18

Select the object you want to click to begin the trigger animation. Renaming objects in the Selection and Visibility pane helps you select the right one in this drop-down list.

Apply Exit Animation

We want the information shape to go away when you click it, so we'll add an exit trigger animation, too. Just follow these steps:

1. On the slide, select the shape with the information about the February 5 game. In the Custom Animation pane, choose Add Effect, Exit, and Disappear. If Disappear doesn't show up in the list, choose More Effects.

2. Click the down arrow next to the exit animation in the Custom Animation pane and choose Timing to open the dialog box for the exit animation.

3. On the Timing tab in the animation's dialog box, click the Triggers button, and then choose Start Effect on Click Of. In the drop-down box, select the item you want to click to start the animation (see Figure 7.19). We've chosen feb5 info; now when we click the feb5 info shape, it will disappear.

Figure 7.19

The object with the February 5 game information has two animations applied. One is an entrance animation, which is triggered when you click the feb5 basketball clip art. The other is an exit animation that is triggered when you click the feb5 info shape itself.

Repeat the previous two sections to create shapes and apply entrance and exit trigger animations for the basketball games on February 13 and 27 and for the play at the theater on February 10. Information for these events can be found on slides 5, 7, and 8. The final slide should look similar to Figure 7.20.

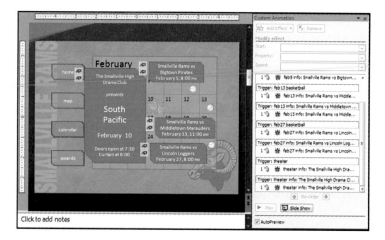

Figure 7.20
All information shapes have been created, and entrance and exit trigger animations have been applied to each.

Set Up Kiosk Mode

Sometimes when users are trying to click buttons or objects on slides, they click the slide itself by mistake, which usually makes the presentation advance to the next slide. If you want your users to rely only on the buttons and navigation links you've provided, set your presentation to Kiosk mode.

To do this, click the Slide Show tab on the Ribbon, and then choose Set Up Slide Show. This opens the Set Up Show dialog box, where you can choose Browsed At a Kiosk. Now your presentation won't move to another slide unless users click the navigation buttons specifically.

Step 5.   Create the Awards Slide

The last tasks in this makeover are very simple: Make the Awards slide look better than just a bulleted text list, and delete the extra slides.

If you are following the makeover step by step, just continue using your saved presentation. If you just stepped in, you can use the **kiosk_04.pptx** presentation from the Makeover 06\Steps folder on the CD.

To make the Awards slide look better, follow these steps:

1. Make sure that slide 4 is the active slide. Select the Home tab on the Ribbon; then in the Drawing Group, click the Shapes button. In the Shapes gallery, choose Wave from the Stars and Banner section and click and drag on the slide to create a wave shape.

2. Type **Regional Show Choir** in the shape; then right-click the shape and choose 24 point from the drop-down list on the mini toolbar.

3. Select the shape and click the Drawing Tools Format tab on the Ribbon; then in the Shape Effects group, choose Bevel, Circle.

4. Click the Home tab on the Ribbon; then in the Drawing group, click the Shapes button and choose the Text Box from the Basic Shapes section of the gallery. Click the slide and type #1. Right-click the text box and choose 48 point from the drop-down list on the mini toolbar.

5. Select the text box and choose the Drawing Tools Format tab on the Ribbon and then WordArt Styles, Fill: White, Warm Matte Bevel (see Figure 7.21). Click and drag the text box just above the text in the Wave shape. Select the shape and the text box and drag them to the top of the slide (see Figure 7.23, a bit later).

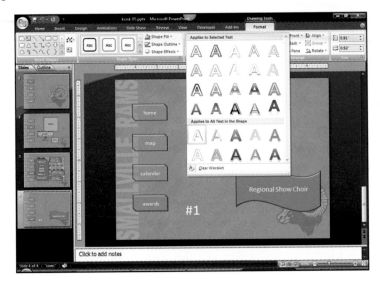

Figure 7.21

The Quick Style galleries let you apply awesome formatting options with just one click.

6. Repeat steps 1 through 5 for the other two awards listed on slide 9 (see Figure 7.22).

Finally, delete slides 5 through 9 because they're no longer needed. That's good, because they sure were ugly! If you'd like to see the completed presentation, open `kiosk_05.pptx` file from the Makeover 06\Steps folder on the CD.

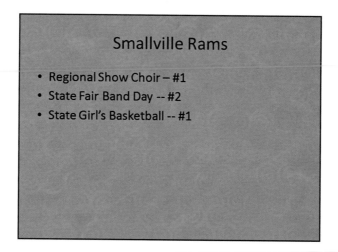

Figure 7.22

The Awards slide before…

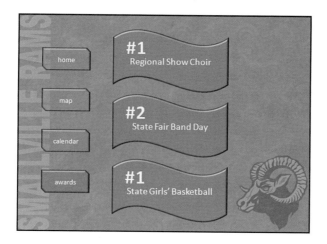

Figure 7.23

…and after.

meet henry

- a.k.a mr. MBA
- henry lives in seattle
- he drives a nice car
- and loves coffee

Before

meet **henry**

After

8

Makeover 7: No Bullets Presentation

YOU WILL LEARN HOW TO:

- Apply a Clean Theme
- Promote Bullets to Slide Titles
- Change the Slide Layout
- Make Do with Fewer Words
- Add Visuals
- Play with Text Formatting

About This Makeover

For this makeover, I used an award-winning presentation created by the team of Scott Schwertly and Cheree Moore at Ethos3 Communications (www.ethos3.com). I wish to thank them for allowing me to use their presentation.

Unlike in other makeovers in this book, this presentation is a concept makeover rather than a new-features-in-PowerPoint makeover.

This presentation uses no bullets, and often uses pictures instead of words to create "concept slides." A picture of a cup of coffee represents coffee much better than just the word "coffee" because so much more is visible in a picture: There's the cup, the froth in the coffee, and the color of the coffee itself. Thus pictures engage the audience— people can form their own stories, and they will pay more attention to the presentation because they are more involved this way.

The way you present your message can be more important than the message itself. This is especially true if you want to use PowerPoint to illustrate a concept rather than just show some numbers. True, this no-bullets style of presentation might not be suitable (or even possible) all the time, but if you used this style all the time, it might not be as effective. Thus, the secret is to use this style in the opening or closing slides of a conventional presentation, and when the situation permits, you also can use it in an entire presentation, as we did in this makeover.

Remember that this presentation style does not reduce the number of slides you'll have to make—every slide that includes a title and four bullet points now must be changed to five slides: one for the title and one concept slide for each individual bullet!

Figure 8.1 shows you the "before" sample slides. Although the text looks crisp and clear, the presentation itself lacks life because it tries to tell a story using just a few words. The words that are used get lost because there are so many of them on a single slide, and I haven't even come to the visuals yet.

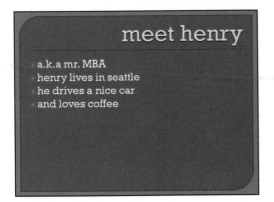 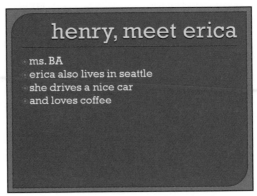

Figure 8.1
These were created using one of the built-in design themes contained in PowerPoint 2007.

To see how much difference a few words and visuals can make, go no further than Figure 8.2. This is the same content presented in slides that build on each other using a story sequence style.

Figure 8.2
Nothing more, nothing less, and just enough!

Step 1.   Apply a Clean Theme

The first thing you need to do to make over this presentation is apply a clean theme or template. A *clean* theme is a simple slide design that includes a plain white background—think of it as an empty canvas. Applying a clean theme allows the pictures to stand out well. To apply the theme, follow these steps:

1. Open the **nobullets_00.pptx** presentation from the Makeover 07\Steps folder on the CD.

2. Click the Design tab on the Ribbon, and mouse over the themes that you see in Figure 8.3. Click on the theme thumbnail when the ToolTip says Office Theme. Even if you can't see the ToolTips, this theme is easy to locate because it's the only one that has a plain white background.

3. All the slides in the presentation now will show a white background. Save your presentation.

Themes are found in the Theme gallery.

Each theme has a name (see ToolTip).

Figure 8.3

Apply a clean theme.

Step 2.   Create a Slide from Each Bullet

Because you want text on every slide kept to a minimum, you really can't have four or five bullets on each slide. Thus, we are going to make all those bullets into individual slides; the bullets themselves will get promoted to slide titles. That's the best promotion any bullet can get!

If you are following the makeover step by step, continue using your saved presentation. If you just stepped in, you can use the **nobullets_01.pptx** presentation from the Makeover 07\Steps folder on the CD.

Follow these steps:

1. Make sure that the Home tab on the Ribbon is active. Click the Outline tab of the Slides pane so that you can see the entire text outline of the presentation, as shown in Figure 8.4.

2. As you can see in Figure 8.4, there are way too many bullets in the slides. On the Outline pane, select all the bullets on one of the slides (see Figure 8.5), and press Shift+Tab on your keyboard (see Figure 8.6).

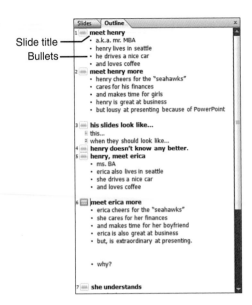

Slide title ———

Bullets ———

Figure 8.4

The outline is here.

Before   After

Figure 8.5

Promoting bullets to slide titles.

3. Lo and behold, all those bullets now are individual slide titles (see the "after" image in Figure 8.5). Repeat step 2 for all the bullets in the rest of the slides to end up with a presentation bereft of bullets. The 9-slide presentation now has 35 slides and may have still more by the time we are done.

4. Save the presentation.

Step 3.   Change the Slide Layout

Because we have almost no text other than the slide titles on any slide, it makes no sense to retain the Slide Layout that includes bulleted text. So now I'll show you how you can change the layout of all slides to the Title Only layout.

If you are following the makeover step by step, continue using your saved presentation. If you just stepped in, you can use the **nobullets_02.pptx** presentation from the Makeover 07\Steps folder on the CD.

Follow these steps:

1. Click the View tab on the Ribbon, and click Slide Sorter. This shows all the slides in Slide Sorter view, and you can see the presentation as thumbnails (see Figure 8.6).

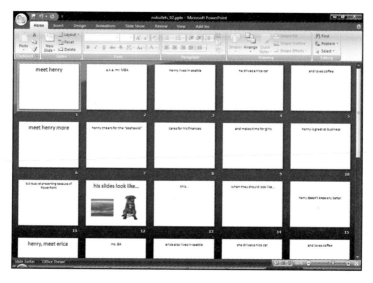

Figure 8.6

All thumbnails represent slides.

2. Press Ctrl+A to select all the slides in the view, click the Home tab on the Ribbon, and click the Layout button to view the Layout gallery that you can see in Figure 8.7.

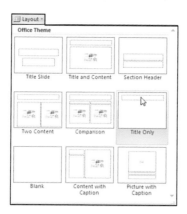

Figure 8.7

A drop-down gallery of layouts makes it easy to change Slide Layouts.

3. Click the Title Only thumbnail (refer to Figure 8.7). This will change the layout of all selected slides in the presentation to Title Only.

4. To view the presentation in the conventional edit mode, click the View tab on the Ribbon, and click Normal. Save the presentation.

Step 4.   Consolidate the Slides

In the previous steps of this makeover, all the bullets were promoted to slide titles, and the Slide Layout for all the slides in the presentation was changed. Yet, there's always some housekeeping left that cannot be done automatically with a click or two. If you are following the steps in this makeover, or doing another makeover on your own, remember to look out for any problem areas that need attention. The sooner you spot these problems in the makeover process, the easier they are to resolve.

There are several ways to find out whether there are problem areas in a presentation, but two of them are time-tested and indispensable:

■ Play your presentation from the first slide to the last several times.

■ Look closely at the presentation in Outline view.

You are sure to discover a few things that you want to correct after you review the presentation. In the case of our current makeover, I discovered many empty lines in the outline between slides 26 and 35 (see Figure 8.8). I also discovered that slide 34 had two titles!

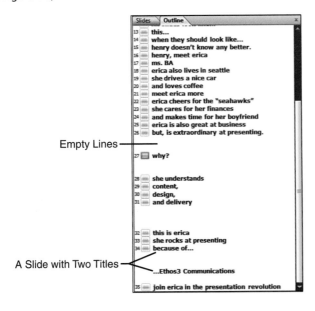

Figure 8.8

The outline makes it easy to spot goof-ups.

If you are following the makeover step by step, continue using your saved presentation. If you just stepped in, you can use the `nobullets_03.pptx` presentation from the `Makeover 07\Steps` folder on the CD.

Follow these steps to sort out the issues:

1. In the Slides pane, click the Outline tab to view the outline (refer to Figure 8.8). Slides 1–25 seem perfectly fine; each slide has a single-line title. However, look what happens after slide 26. You need to make some changes here.

2. Click in the Outline tab, right after the end of the sentence in Slide 26. Press the Delete key twice (or thrice, if required) to get rid of those empty lines. If you pressed the Delete key once too often, quickly press Ctrl+Z to undo.

3. Repeat the process for slides 27 and 31.

4. For slide 34, you need to take another approach. This slide has two lines that should have been distributed as two titles in successive slides. Fortunately, that's exactly the type of task that takes a mere moment to fix in the Outline tab.

   Click at the end of the first title line ("because of…"), and press the Delete key twice so that there are no empty lines between the first and second lines of the title, as shown in Figure 8.9.

Before　　　　　　　　　　　　　　　After

Figure 8.9

Create new slides in the outline.

5. Press the Delete key once again and then, press Enter. Now the lines are on two separate slides. Next, remove the extra line in the title on the newly created slide to end up with what you see in the "after" image in Figure 8.9.

6. Save your presentation.

Step 5.   Add More Slides

Now that you have consolidated the slides, it's time to add some more! I'll be showing you how you can divide one slide into two. Even after these two slides are separated, they maintain a link because they share a text-to-visual relationship. That might sound very impressive, but in fact, it is something so simple that even a kindergartener could probably understand it.

Let's look at this title: henry lives in seattle.

Now break this into two slides:

- First slide: henry lives in
- Second slide: seattle.

Now remove the word "seattle" altogether from the second slide, and insert in its place a large picture of the Seattle skyline that includes the Space Needle. Now even if you don't put the word "Seattle" in the title, everybody still knows that Seattle is what the picture portrays. The before and after of this concept can be seen in Figure 8.10.

Figure 8.10
One slide becomes two slides.

We'll put in all those pictures later; for now, let's start splitting the slides. If you are following the makeover step by step, continue using your saved presentation. If you just stepped in, you can use the **nobullets_04.pptx** presentation from the Makeover 07\Steps folder on the CD.

Follow these steps:

1. Divide the second slide (a.k.a. Mr.MBA) into two slides; the two new titles will be "a.k.a." and "Mr. MBA".

2. You need to do the same thing with many other slides, but for now, you can just open the **nobullets_05.pptx** presentation from the Makeover 07\Steps folder on the CD, which contains the split slides. In fact, take a look at how I split the slides in **nobullets_05.pptx**, and replicate that in your presentation.

   You will notice that some slides such as "Meet Henry More" were deleted because they no longer serve a purpose. In addition, some slides were split into more than two slides; look at the **nobullets_05.pptx** presentation to get an idea of the changes made.

TIP

You can split slides quickly in the Outline pane by pressing Enter in the middle of a title to create a new slide from the second half of the title.

---

3. Remove the two pictures in the erstwhile slide 12.
4. Save the presentation.

Step 6.   Add Pictures

This is both the most difficult and the easiest part of the makeover.

The difficult part is in finding and choosing appropriate photos. Remember, it is better not to use a photo than try to use one that's not relevant or suitable. In addition, never use two or more photos if you can get the message across with just one. You'll only end up confusing the viewer and crowding the slide.

The easy part is inserting the pictures. It takes a mere two clicks to do that!

Before I start showing how you can insert photos, a few words on copyright issues won't hurt.

RESPECTING COPYRIGHTS

This is not a topic that can be covered in its entirety here. In fact, there are books dedicated to only this subject. However, it does not take a master's degree in rocket science to understand how you can respect copyrights. These few guidelines will help:

- Start with exploring your own resources. Many times, you can use your own digital camera to click photographs for use in your presentations. Even then, there may be some copyright issues involved if you are shooting pictures of private property (or even shooting pictures while you are within private property).

- Most stock photo sites won't have problems with you using their photos in a presentation as long as you don't distribute those presentations without a proper license. Licenses can be of several types; always ask the stock photo site from which you bought the photo for details.

- Never copy photographs from a website unless you have requested and received permission.

- Whenever in doubt, it's best to ask.

If you are following the makeover step by step, continue using your saved presentation. If you just stepped in, you can use the **nobullets_05.pptx** presentation from the Makeover 07\Steps folder on the CD.

Follow these steps to insert your pictures:

1. Locate the pictures subfolder of the Makeover 07 folder on the CD, where you'll find several pictures all named with the slide number reference where they have to be inserted.

TIP

Although you also can navigate to the folder on the CD when inserting the pictures, you might want to copy these pictures off the CD to your computer to make locating them easier.

2. With the first slide of the presentation open, click the Insert tab on the Ribbon, and choose Picture. The Insert Picture dialog box opens, as shown in Figure 8.11.

Navigate to the folder that contains the pictures.

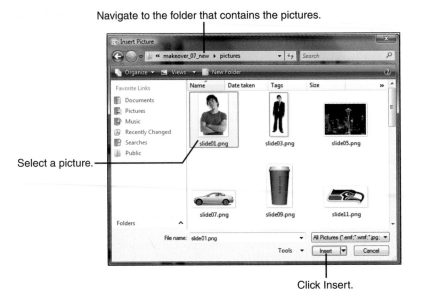

Select a picture.

Click Insert.

Figure 8.11
Insert pictures into slides.

3. Select the first picture (**slide01.png**), and click the Insert button. PowerPoint places the picture on the first slide. Drag the corners of the picture and reposition it so that it doesn't cover the slide title (see Figure 8.12).

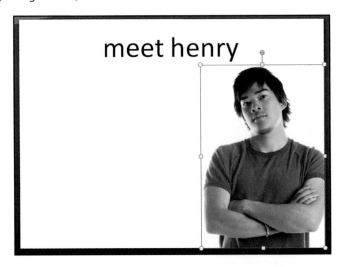

Figure 8.12
Resize and position the picture so it doesn't cover the slide title.

4. Repeat this process for the remaining slides. Some slides don't have any pictures. That's okay; just leave them for now.

5. Save the presentation.

Step 7.   Work with the Titles and Slide Backgrounds

Now that we have the actual slides in place and the pictures inserted, it's time to work with the titles. Essentially, this entails two tasks:

1. Remove titles where they are not required. For example, remove them from slides that have visuals. A cup of coffee is so recognizable that you don't need to add a title that says "coffee"!

2. Format and position the titles. This comprises making some words bold and maybe moving the location of the title to a different part of the slide. Because there's no single fixed position for the title in these slides, we need not work with any of the Slide Layouts within the Slide Master.

NOTE

Working with Slide Layouts and the Slide Master are covered fully in Chapter 6, "Makeover 5: Halloween Scrapbook."

In addition, there are plenty of slides that have no pictures. However, they do have titles. We'll change the slide backgrounds of those slides to black, and we'll change the title text to white.

If you are following the makeover step by step, continue using your saved presentation. If you just stepped in, you can use the **nobullets_06.pptx** presentation from the Makeover 07\Steps folder on the CD.

Now that you know what has to be done, do the following to get started:

1. Click the View tab on the Ribbon, and select Slide Sorter to view the slides in Slide Sorter view.

2. Press Ctrl and click all the slides that have no pictures, to select them.

3. Now click the Design tab on the Ribbon, and click Background Styles to see the Background Styles gallery. Right-click the black thumbnail on the top row, and in the resulting menu, click the Apply to Selected Slides option (see Figure 8.13).

   Not only does this cause all the backgrounds within the selected slides to turn black, but also it changes the title text on all these slides to white.

4. Now click the View tab on the Ribbon, and click Normal. Go to Slide 1, and select **Henry** in the title. This should bring up the mini toolbar that contains almost all the text formatting options you might need (see Figure 8.14). If the mini toolbar does not pop up, you can right-click the selected text to summon it. Click the Bold option in the mini toolbar to make the selected text bold. Now you have a title that's partially bold.

Figure 8.13

Change the background style of slides.

TIP

How do you decide which part of the title needs to be bold? Most of the time, this would be the more important word in the title. We think Henry is more important in this title than Meet, and thus chose to make that bold. Of course, this is really open to your creative freedom.

Figure 8.14

Do your text formatting with the mini toolbar.

5. Reposition the title "meet henry" anywhere that you find appropriate on the slide (see Figure 8.15).

Figure 8.15

Playing with the slide titles feels like breaking rules, but it can be fun!

TIP

Normally I would not suggest that you move around your slide titles this way (after all, that's akin to behaving as if there's no Slide Master or Slide Layout in PowerPoint). So why do it now? Because you need some creative freedom at times, and rules certainly can be broken as long as you are aware of what they are in the first place. And remember, this is an advertising presentation, not something intended for a board meeting—that itself allows for more freedom.

---

6. Using the suggestions in the previous steps, go ahead and alter the remaining slides to your liking. Here is a list of some other stuff that I did to our sample makeover:

   ■ Removed the titles for slides that don't need them; these include the slides that have a picture of a car, coffee, or Seattle.

   ■ Added ellipses to the end of some phrases to provide a sense of continuation between text and picture slides. So if the text in one slide was "Henry lives in…," the second slide had a picture of Seattle to complete the thought.

   ■ Moved the titles to various positions, including at the bottom of the slide, so that the title in some slides was placed away from the pictures. Really, this sort of decision is based more on the picture within a slide and how it copes visually with the accompanying title. Indeed, there's a method to this madness, but it's also a combination of several things that might require an entire book to explain. We suggest you look at billboards, television ads, movie posters, and so on, and observe how they place the text in relation to the visuals (or even on an empty expanse), and try to replicate that. Practice makes perfect!

   ■ Moved the location of pictures, too. This again followed no rules. Every slide is different, and every picture is distinctive—you need to see what works best in a given scenario. For example, if the picture is of a boy looking toward the left, we'll move him to the right side of the slide so that he can look inside the slide area rather than outside. Many of these ideas are inspired by photography techniques—look up concepts such as the "rule of thirds" in a photography composition book to learn more. You also can learn much by just observing more slides and photographs.

   Your presentation doesn't have to look exactly like mine, but you can take a look at the **nobullets_07.pptx** presentation from the `Makeover 07\Steps` folder on the CD to get an idea of what I did.

7. Save your presentation.

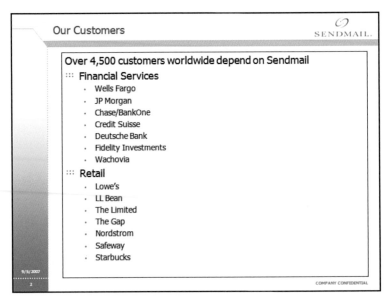

Before

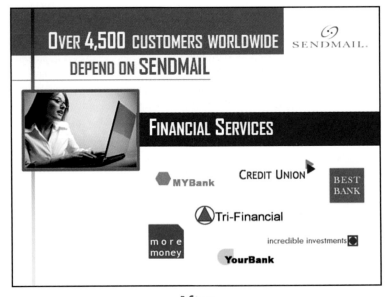

After

ON THE CD:

The sample presentation and all other files with which you need to work can be found on the CD in the `Makeover 08` folder.

9

Makeover 8: Trade Show Loop Presentation

YOU WILL LEARN HOW TO:

- Work with Custom Animation
- Use the Selection and Visibility Pane
- Add Background Music
- Make Your Presentation Loop

About This Makeover

When you're exhibiting at a tradeshow, your presentation must command attention. After all, you want people to stop and watch it.

Stand-alone presentations are different from the typical, speaker-led presentation for obvious reasons: they do stand alone, and they don't need to support a speaker. In fact, in many ways, they *are* the speaker.

One way to grab the eye of a passerby is to kick up the animation. Make that stuff *move*! While lots of motion might be inappropriate during a typical presentation, in a tradeshow-type loop, it's more than appropriate—it's vital!

To increase the impact of this presentation, we inserted graphics and other visuals, used minimal text, and added sophisticated animation. Finally, we added background music to pump up the impact and create a full media effect. Make sure your booth has speakers!

This makeover is based on a more complete makeover by designer Julie Terberg, who also is the technical editor for this book. We had to scale it down for space considerations, so to get the full benefit of her work, we encourage you to take a look at the complete file—and others—in Julie's online portfolio at http://www.terbergdesign.com.

Step 1. Set Up Theme Colors and Slide Master

Open the original presentation, `loop_00.pptx`, by clicking Office Button, Open. This file can be found on the CD in the `Makeover 08\Steps` folder.

The original presentation is a typical, bulleted slide presentation. While that's fine for draft content, we want to use bold, eye-grabbing graphics for the tradeshow loop. Thus, we'll start a completely new file, rather than spend time trying to bend this original to our needs. You can see the "before" and "after" looks in Figures 9.1 and 9.2.

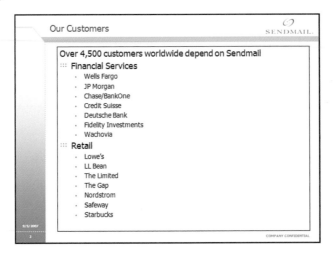

Figure 9.1

This boring bulleted slide....

Figure 9.2

...becomes two high-impact slides.

KNOW YOUR ASPECT RATIO

Many tradeshow presentations are displayed on wide screens, and it's important to know the aspect ratio of the screen before you design the presentation.

The default PowerPoint presentation has a 4×3 aspect ratio, but wide-screen displays usually are 16×9 or 16×10. You can change this setting by clicking the Design tab on the Ribbon and then clicking Page Setup.

Beware! If you change your page size from one aspect ratio to another, the existing graphics on the slides will be distorted. There's no automatic way to correct this—you're just in for a lot of tedious manual resizing.

Here's a list of what we did to create a new starting file:

1. First, we created a new theme color set. The red and the steel are based on colors in the logo; navy blue was added to give us a complementary color to work with.

2. We positioned the title placeholder and created a subtitle placeholder on the Title and Content and Title Only layouts. Then we deleted extraneous layouts.

3. We created a Theme Font set, using Agency FB for the heading font to give the file a techno feel and Trebuchet MS for body text (which we won't really need in this abbreviated makeover).

4. We formatted the title font as white. We will place a red rectangle beneath it to frame the title, but because we want to animate those rectangles, we need to add them to the individual slides and not to the Slide Master or Slide Layouts. In fact, most of our objects will be added directly to the slide, so our Slide Master looks pretty empty!

5. Finally, we specified small caps for the title text so that we wouldn't have to worry about the letters overlapping the bottom edge of the framing rectangle.

At this point you have a white background on the slides, and because there's no text or anything else, you cannot really see the fonts or the colors. That's precisely why we did not provide a figure to look at!

However, you can open the **loop_01.pptx** from the Makeover 08\Steps folder on the CD, and explore the Theme Fonts and Theme Color choices.

Step 2. Prepare the Logo for Animation

Our first step is to make sure the product logo is big and bold and that it captures attention. We'll add some rectangles to the slide to help frame the logo; then we'll animate the entire logo to make sure it's noticed.

To follow along in this makeover, you can apply the **tradeshowloop.thmx** theme to a new, blank presentation, or you can open the **loop_01.pptx** presentation from the Makeover 08\Steps folder on the CD.

TIP

To apply a new theme to a blank presentation, just double-click the `tradeshowloop.thmx` file on the CD, and save the resulting PowerPoint files as a new presentation.

Add Shapes to Frame the Logo

Apply a blank Slide Layout to the first slide by clicking the Home tab on the Ribbon and then clicking Slides, Layout, Blank.

To create shapes to frame the logo, follow these steps:

1. On the Home tab, go to the Drawing group and click Shapes, Rectangle. Click and drag the width of the slide to create a rectangle.

2. On the Drawing Tools Format tab, type **1.25** into the Height size box, and then press Enter to make the rectangle 1.25" tall.

3. Choose Shape Outline, No Outline. Select and drag the rectangle so that it anchors to the top part of the slide (see Figure 9.3).

4. Press Ctrl+C to copy the rectangle and Ctrl+V to paste. On the Drawing Tools Format tab, choose Shape Fill, Dark Blue Accent 2. Drag the blue shape to the bottom of the slide (see Figure 9.3).

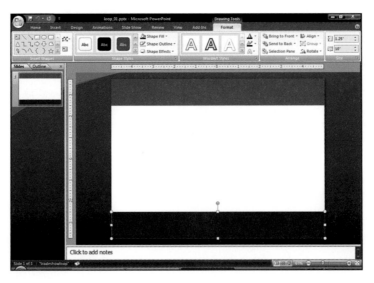

Figure 9.3

Add rectangles to frame the logo.

Crop and Align the Logo and Shapes

We want to animate the product logo in two pieces, so we'll have to insert it onto the slide, size it, copy it, and crop each piece.

You can copy the logo from the Slide Master in the `loop_00.pptx` file, but we also included the logo image file on the CD for your convenience.

To insert the logo onto the slide, click the Insert tab on the Ribbon, click Picture, and then choose the `sendmail-logo.png` file in the Makeover 08\Pictures folder on the CD. Click Insert to add it to the slide.

After the logo is on the slide, follow these steps:

1. Press the Shift key while you click and drag one corner of the logo with your mouse until it's approximately 7.25" wide so that it covers a large part of the slide's width. Pressing Shift constrains the proportions so the logo doesn't become distorted.

2. Press Ctrl+C to copy the logo, and then press Ctrl+V to paste the copy onto the slide.

3. Select one of the logos; then, on the Picture Tools Format tab, click the Crop button and click and drag one of the black handles to crop the image to include just the text. Repeat for the other logo, dragging each edge to crop out the text and leave just the icon (see Figure 9.4).

Drag to crop to just the icon

Figure 9.4

Use the Crop tool to crop out unwanted portions of images.

4. Select both the logo text and the logo icon, and click the Picture Tools Format tab; then, in the Arrange group, click Align to Slide (see Figure 9.5). This tells PowerPoint that you want the objects to be positioned relative to the slide edges.

To align the selected items with the center of the slide, on the Picture Tools Format tab on the Ribbon, in the Arrange group, click Align Center (see Figure 9.5 again).

5. Save the presentation.

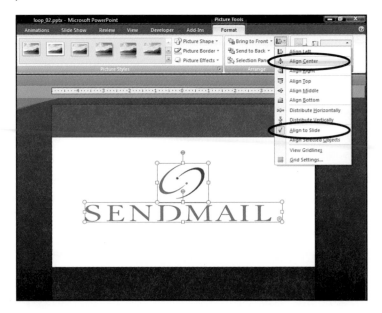

Figure 9.5

The Alignment tools are useful for centering objects on a slide. Just check the Align to Slide option before choosing the position to align them.

Step 3. Animate the Logo

If you are following the makeover step by step, continue using your saved presentation. If you just stepped in, you can use the **loop_02.pptx** presentation from the Makeover 08\Steps folder on the CD.

Now all we have to do is animate the logo pieces! Here's how:

1. Click the Animations tab, and then click Custom Animation. The Custom Animation pane opens.

2. Select the logo icon, and in the Custom Animation pane, choose Add Effect, Entrance, More Effects to bring up the More Effects dialog box. In the Moderate category, select Grow & Turn (see Figure 9.6). Click OK to close the dialog box.

3. In the Custom Animation pane, select the animation and change the Start setting to With Previous.

Figure 9.6

Select any animation effect to preview it on the selected object.

4. Repeat steps 2 and 3 for the logo text image. In step 2, choose Expand (in the Subtle category) instead of Grow & Turn.

Now let's make the dots in the logo glow:

1. Draw a small circle over the red circle in the logo icon. (You might want to zoom to 400% while you do this part. Use the convenient zoom slider on the status bar.) The default circle has an outline, but the circle will be so small on the slide you won't be able to tell it's a different color than the fill. If you want, go to the Drawing Tools Format tab on the Ribbon, choose Shape Outline, and select Dark Red, Accent 1 so the outline and fill match.

TIP

If you're having trouble putting objects where you want them, press the Alt key to override the Snap to Grid settings while you drag the object into place.

---

2. On the Home tab of the Ribbon, go to the Editing group and click Select, Selection Pane. Then double-click the word Oval in the pane and type **Red Circle** to rename the object.

3. Select the red circle on the slide, and on the Custom Animation pane, choose Add Effect, Entrance, Appear. Change the Start setting to After Previous (see Figure 9.7).

TIP

If the Custom Animation pane is not visible, summon it by clicking the Animations tab on the ribbon, and then clicking the Custom Animation button.

---

4. With the red circle still selected on the slide, choose Add Effect and then Emphasis, More Effects, Grow/Shrink (see Figure 9.7). Change the Start setting to With Previous, the Size setting to Custom 400%, and the Speed setting to Very Fast.

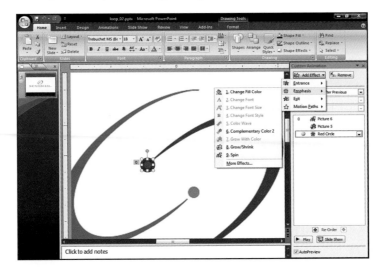

Figure 9.7

Select an object on the slide, and you can add multiple animation effects using the Add Effect button.

NOTE

When you select an object on the slide, the first button in the Custom Animation pane will be Add Effect. If you select the animation effect in the Custom Animation pane, that same button will read Change. It will be Change because you must choose an existing effect in the pane to modify the animation, but if you select the object on the slide, you can add *more* animation effects to it.

---

5. Again, with the circle selected on the slide, choose Add Effect, then Exit, More Effects, Fade. Change the Start setting to With Previous and the Speed setting to Very Fast.

6. Press Ctrl+C to copy the circle, and then press Ctrl+V three times to add three more animated circles. Your slide and custom animation pane should look similar to Figure 9.8 now.

7. Select one of the copies of the red circle and rename it to `Blue Circle` in the Selection and Visibility pane (refer to step 2). Change the Shape Fill and Shape Outline colors (on the Drawing Tools Format tab, in the Shape Styles group) to Blue-Gray Accent 3.

8. Paste two copies of the animated blue circle onto the slide.

9. Align the three red circles on top of the red circle in the logo, and then align the three blue circles on top of the blue (teal) circle on the logo.

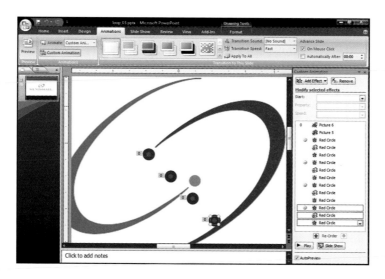

Figure 9.8

Copies of animated objects have the same animations already applied.

10. In the Custom Animation pane, press the Shift key and click to choose the last three Blue Circle animations. Click the Re-Order up arrow to move this set of animations so that they occur just after the first set of red circle animations. Move another set of blue animations to occur after the second set of red animations. When you finish, your Custom Animation pane should look like the one shown in Figure 9.9.

Figure 9.9

Use the Re-Order buttons to reorder animations in the Custom Animation pane.

11. Right-click an animation in the pane and choose Show Advanced Timeline.

12. Click and drag the orange triangle for the second red circle entrance animation to add a one-second delay between its appearance and the end of the previous animation. Drag its associated emphasis and exit animations to the same start point. Repeat for the last red circle (see Figure 9.10).

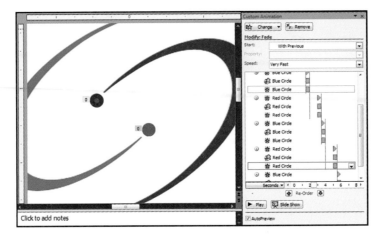

Figure 9.10

The Custom Animation pane shows the advanced timeline. You can click and drag the orange shapes to adjust animations.

13. Click the Play button at the bottom of the Custom Animation pane to preview the animation sequence you created.

USING THE ADVANCED ANIMATION TIMELINE

Right-click any animation in the Custom Animation pane and choose Show Advanced Timeline to see a graphic representation of the animation sequence for the slide.

The Advanced Timeline shows how your objects are animating. Drag the edge of the timeline to make it wider. You also can click the Seconds button and choose Zoom In to see the timings more closely.

Clicking and dragging on any of the orange timing shapes (think of sliders) lets you move it on the timeline, effectively creating or eliminating delays between objects (see Figure 9.11).

Clicking and dragging the left or right edge of any of the orange bars in the timeline lets you change the duration of the animation (see Figure 9.12).

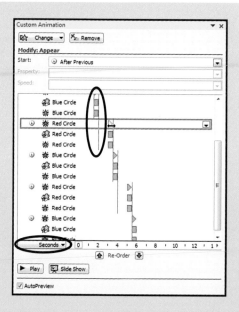

Figure 9.11

When your cursor turns to a horizontal arrow, you can drag an animation into place on the timeline.

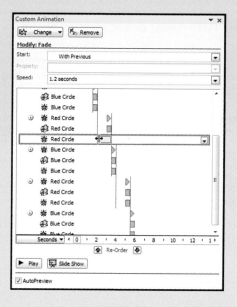

Figure 9.12

When your cursor turns to this vertical crosshair, you can drag the start or end time to change the duration of the animation effect.

The black vertical lines you see in the Advanced Timeline are created when you set an animation to Start After Previous. The line marks the "previous" animation and prevents you from moving the start point for subsequent animations before that line (refer to Figure 9.11).

If you prefer to work by the numbers, you can double-click any animation in the Custom Animation pane to open the Effect Options dialog box. On the Timing tab, type the delay time and speed (duration) you want to use (see Figure 9.13).

Figure 9.13
Double-click any animation effect in the Custom Animation pane to type specific delay times or animation speeds.

Step 4. Create and Animate a Message Slide

One of the main messages of this presentation is that 4,500 customers depend on Sendmail, but this message is buried on a bulleted list slide in the original presentation. We'll create a slide to highlight that statement and set up the next couple of slides.

If you are following the makeover step by step, continue using your saved presentation. If you just stepped in, you can use the `loop_03.pptx` presentation from the `Makeover 08\Steps` folder on the CD.

Add Graphics to a Copy of a Slide

Because some of the graphics we need are already on slide 1, we'll duplicate the slide instead of starting from scratch, and then add more graphics. Follow these steps:

1. Select slide 1 in the Slides pane, press Ctrl+D to duplicate the slide. Click the Fit Slide to Current Window button on the status bar so that you can see the entire slide in the workspace (see Figure 9.14).

Figure 9.14

Click the Fit Slide to Current Window button so you can see the entire slide in the workspace.

2. With slide 2 selected in the Slides pane, click the Home tab, go to the Slides group, and click Layout, Title Only. Title and subtitle placeholders will appear on the slide.

3. Type the message into the title and subtitle placeholders (see Figure 9.15). Change the font color of the word Sendmail to red (on the Home tab, in the Font group, click the Text Color drop-down arrow, and choose the red color in the Theme Colors section) to make it stand out. You might need to change the font size of the subtitle placeholder to 42 (on the Home tab, in the Font group, click the Font Size drop-down arrow).

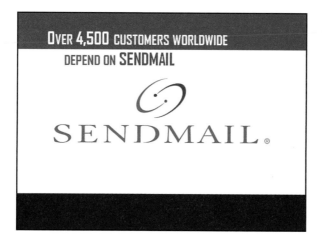

Figure 9.15

Type the message in the title placeholders.

TIP

If you're using lowercase or sentence-case text on your slides, consider putting the product name in small caps to help it stand out.

4. Select all the logo pieces and click the Home tab on the Ribbon; then, in the Drawing group, click Arrange, Group. This removes all animation from the logo.

5. On the Home tab of the Ribbon, in the Drawing group click Shapes, and then click Line. Click and drag to draw a vertical line near the left edge of the slide. This helps anchor the title text. You can see the position of the line in Figure 9.16.

6. With the line selected, click the Drawing Tools Format tab; then, in the Shape Styles group, click Shape Outline, Weight, More Lines. This opens the Format Shape dialog box. Click Line Style on the left, and then type 7 in the Line Width box.

7. Click the Line Color option in the Format Shape dialog box and choose Gradient Line.

8. In the Direction list box, choose Linear Down, and change the Angle setting to 0. Select Stop 1 in the Gradient stops section, and change its color to Dark Blue Accent 2. Change the Gradient stop to Stop 3 and change its color to Dark Blue Accent 2 Lighter 90% (see Figure 9.16).

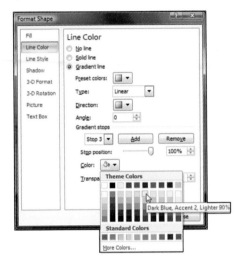

Figure 9.16

Change gradient colors here.

9. Select Stop 2 in the Gradient stops section, and click the Remove button to delete the middle gradient color. This allows us to set only the beginning (stop 1) and end (stop 2) colors of the gradient and let PowerPoint do the rest of the work!

10. On the Home tab of the Ribbon, in the Drawing group, click Shapes, and then click Line. Click and drag from the left edge to the center of the slide to draw a small horizontal line to anchor the subtitle. On the Drawing Tools Format tab of the Ribbon, use the Shape Outline settings to give it a 1.5 pt weight and a Blue-Gray Accent 3 color (see Figure 9.17).

11. Save your presentation.

Figure 9.17
Specify various line settings using the options in Shape Outline.

Add Animation

Our slide has a linear look, so we'll keep the animation linear as well. We'll slide the blue rectangle off the bottom and slide the red rectangle off the left; we'll then move the logo diagonally to the upper-right corner.

If you are following the makeover step by step, continue using your saved presentation. If you just stepped in, you can use the **loop_04.pptx** presentation from the Makeover 08\Steps folder on the CD.

Follow these steps:

1. Select the blue rectangle at the bottom of slide 2, and in the Custom Animation pane, choose Add Effect, Exit, More Effects, Fly Out. Change the Start setting to With Previous and the Speed setting to Fast.

2. Select the red rectangle at the top of the slide, and in the Custom Animation pane, choose Add Effect, Motion Path, Left. Change the Start setting to With Previous and the Speed setting to Fast.

3. Select the logo and choose Add Effect, Emphasis, Grow/Shrink. Change the Start setting to With Previous and the Size setting to Custom 27% (See Figure 9.18). Press Tab or Enter on your keyboard to apply the new percentage setting.

Figure 9.18

The Custom Animation pane after applying animation effects to the two rectangles and the logo.

4. Select the logo on the slide and choose Add Effect, Motion Path, More Motion Paths, Up. Change the Start setting to With Previous. Select the handle on the end of the red arrow indicating the end of the motion path, and drag it to the upper-right corner of the slide (see Figure 9.19).

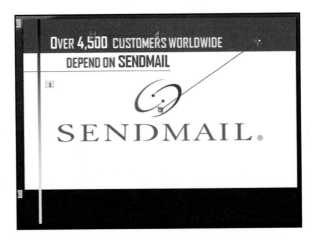

Figure 9.19

Drag the end of a motion path to change its endpoint.

5. If necessary, right-click any animation in the Custom Animation pane and choose Show Advanced Timeline. Drag the logo emphasis and motion path animations bars in the Custom Animation pane so they begin at .7 seconds—before the red and blue rectangles complete their animations (see Figure 9.20).

6. Save your file.

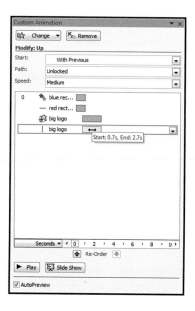

Figure 9.20

Starting an animation With Previous and dragging in the Advanced Animation Timeline of the Custom Animation pane is an easy way to create delays between animations.

TIP

Renaming objects in the Selection and Visibility pane really helps you understand what's animating and when.

If you are following the makeover step by step, continue using your saved presentation. If you just stepped in, you can use the `loop_05.pptx` presentation from the `Makeover 08\Steps` folder on the CD.

1. Select the vertical line on the left side of the slide, and in the Custom Animation pane, choose Add Effect, Entrance More Effects, Fade. Change the Start setting to With Previous and drag the animation bar in the pane so that it begins about half a second before the logo animation completes (see Figure 9.21).

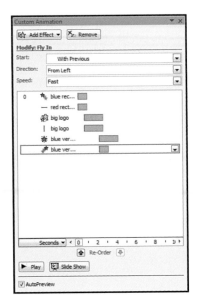

Figure 9.21
The blue vertical line has both fade and fly in animations added to it.

2. With the vertical line selected on the slide, choose Add Effect, Entrance More Effects, Fly In. Change the Start setting to With Previous, the Direction to From Left, and the Speed setting to Fast (see Figure 9.21).

3. Save your file.

If you are following the makeover step by step, continue using your saved presentation. If you just stepped in, you can use the `loop_06.pptx` presentation from the `Makeover 08\Steps` folder on the CD.

1. Select the title placeholder ("Over 4,500 customers worldwide") and add a Fade entrance animation. Change the Start setting to With Previous and the Speed setting to Very Fast. Double-click the animation effect in the Custom Animation pane to open the Fade dialog box. Choose to animate the text By letter, with a 5% delay between letters (see Figure 9.22).

2. Repeat step 8 for the subtitle ("depend on Sendmail"). Drag the animation bar in the timeline so that it begins when the previous text box finishes its animation (see Figure 9.23).

3. Click the Play button at the bottom of the Custom Animation pane to see how your animation looks so far. Save your file.

Figure 9.22

Double-click an effect in the Custom Animation pane to access its options. You also can right-click the effect and choose Effect Options to open this dialog box.

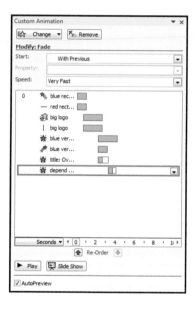

Figure 9.23

The Custom Animation pane looks like this after you apply animations to the text.

If you are following the makeover step by step, continue using your saved presentation. If you just stepped in, you can use the **loop_07.pptx** presentation from the Makeover 08\Steps folder on the CD.

1. Select the horizontal line under the subtitle on slide 2, and add an Appear entrance animation with a Start setting of With Previous. Drag the animation bar in the timeline so that it begins at the same time as the title placeholder (see Figure 9.24).

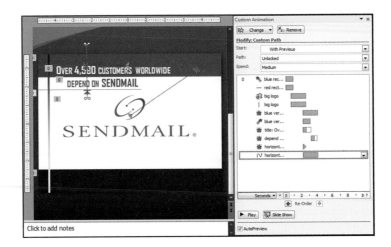

Figure 9.24

The Custom Animation pane looks like this after you apply animations to the text. The lines on the slide with green and red arrowheads indicate motion path animations.

2. Select the horizontal line on the slide and choose Add Effect, Motion Paths, Draw Custom Path, Freeform. Click above the slide to begin the path, click below the line on the slide, and then double-click the line to end the path. This creates a "bounce" effect that emphasizes the subtitle. Change the Start setting to With Previous (refer to Figure 9.24).

3. Click the Play button at the bottom of the Custom Animation pane to see what your animation looks like so far. Save your file.

Finally, we want to add a small logo to sit in the corner of the slide. We must do this because although we want the logo to appear on all the slides, we don't want a big animating logo to occur on each one!

If you are following the makeover step by step, continue using your saved presentation. If you just stepped in, you can use the `loop_08.pptx` presentation from the Makeover 08\Steps folder on the CD.

1. Copy and paste the big logo on slide 2; then, on the Picture Tools Format tab, click the Size dialog launcher. Check the Lock Aspect Ratio check box, and then type `1.9575` in the Width box. (This value is the size of the logo [7.25"] times the Grow/Shrink percentage [27%].)

2. In the Custom Animation pane, right-click the motion path animation effect for the small logo and choose Remove. Choose the Emphasis animation effect, click the Change button, and then click Entrance, Appear.

3. Rename the small logo using the Selection pane on the Home tab of the Ribbon.

4. Drag the small logo into the appropriate place on the upper-right corner of the slide. (It doesn't have to be exact.) Use the Re-Order button on the Custom Animation pane to move this animation so that it occurs just as the motion path for the big logo ends (see Figure 9.25).

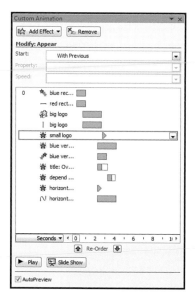

Figure 9.25

The Custom Animation pane looks like this after you create and apply animations to the small logo.

5. Click the Play button at the bottom of the Custom Animation pane to see how your animation looks so far.

6. Save your file.

So we don't have to worry about placing the small logo exactly where the big logo ends, we'll add an exit animation to the big logo. We'll do something similar for the red rectangle at the top of the slide.

If you are following the makeover step by step, continue using your saved presentation. If you just stepped in, you can use the **loop_09.pptx** presentation from the Makeover 08\Steps folder on the CD and continue with these steps to complete the animations.

1. Select the big logo and choose Add Effect, Exit, Disappear. Change the Start setting to With Previous, and use the Re-Order buttons so that this animation occurs next after the small logo animation (see Figure 9.26).

2. Copy and paste the red rectangle onto the slide. Choose its animation effect in the timeline and click Change, Entrance, Appear. Use the Re-Order buttons to move the animation up in the timeline, and drag the animation bar so that it occurs at the end of the original rectangle's animation. Nudge the copy so that it is positioned near where the original red rectangle will be at the end of its animation.

3. Rename the rectangle to #2 Red Rectangle using the Selection and Visibility pane (accessed on the Home tab of the Ribbon by choosing Select, Selection Pane).

4. Select the original red rectangle on the slide and choose Add Effect, Exit, Disappear. Change the Start setting to With Previous and use the Re-Order buttons to move the animation up in the timeline so that it occurs when the short red rectangle appears (see Figure 9.26).

5. Select the short red rectangle and click the Home tab on the Ribbon; then click Arrange, Send to Back so that this object doesn't cover other objects on the slide.

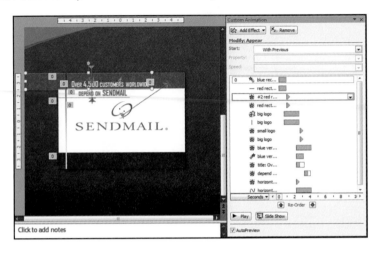

Figure 9.26

The Custom Animation pane looks like this after you apply animations to the copy of the red rectangle, which we named #2 red rectangle. It is selected on the slide.

6. Click the Play button at the bottom of the Custom Animation pane to see what your animation looks like so far. Save your file.

Step 5. Add Some Oomph to Lists of Customers

Customer lists, as you saw in slide 2 of the original presentation, can be boring. To eliminate this boredom, we'll create some slides to really show off who our customers are.

If you are following the makeover step by step, continue using your saved presentation. If you just stepped in, you can use the `loop_10.pptx` presentation from the Makeover 08\Steps folder on the CD.

Add Graphics to a Copy of a Slide

To begin, we'll make a copy of the slide and remove the animation from the existing graphics. Follow these steps:

1. Select slide 2 in the Slides pane, and press Ctrl+D to duplicate the slide.

2. On slide 3, select the original red rectangle that's as wide as the slide, and press the Delete key to delete it. Shorten the remaining red rectangle so that it doesn't hang off the left edge of the slide. Delete the large logo from the middle of the slide.

3. Shift+click the first and last animation effects in the Custom Animation timeline to select all animations; then, click the Remove button at the top of the Custom Animation pane to remove all animation (see Figure 9.27).

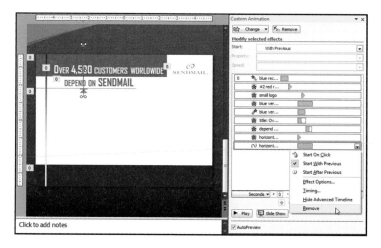

Figure 9.27

Clicking the arrow next to any animation is one way to access options or remove animation effects.

4. Click the Insert tab on the Ribbon and then click Picture to add the corporate logo for each of the financial services companies listed on the original slide. These are in the `Makeover 08\Pictures` folder on the CD.

5. Make the blue rectangle at the bottom of the slide a bit thinner (about 1"), shorten it so that it stops at the vertical line, and move it toward the top of the slide. Copy the title placeholder and type **Financial Services**. Position the text box on the blue rectangle (see Figure 9.28).

6. Because customers really are people, add the picture of the woman at the laptop (`2_2501308.jpg` in the `Makeover 08\Pictures` folder on the CD). Resize it to about 2" tall and add a 6-point red outline.

TIP

Be aware of copyright laws. Royalty-free does not necessarily mean *no cost*. In addition, just because you can download a picture or other media from the Internet doesn't mean you have the right to use it in your presentation. Microsoft Office Online offers completely free photos and sounds for use in your presentation, but if you frequently need photography or music, look into purchasing stock photo and music CDs or subscription packages. The photos of people in this makeover were provided by PhotoSpin (http://www.photospin.com).

Figure 9.28

Logos are more eye-catching than lists of text, and the audience is more likely to remember a logo than just a word. People like to look at other people, so try to add photos of people when you can.

7. Shift+click to select the picture, the blue rectangle, and the Financial Services text, and choose Arrange, Align, Align Middle to vertically center all three pieces (see Figure 9.28). Then choose Arrange, Group to group them. The Align tools are available on the Home tab, the Drawing Tools Format tab, or the Picture Tools Format tab of the Ribbon.

8. Save your file.

Animate the Objects

If you are following the makeover step by step, continue using your saved presentation. If you just stepped in, you can use the `loop_11.pptx` presentation from the `Makeover 08\Steps` folder on the CD and continue with these steps.

Now for the animation! If the Custom Animation pane isn't already visible, click the Animations tab on the Ribbon and then click Custom Animation to open it. Then follow these steps:

1. Make sure you are on slide 3. Select the Financial Services group and in the Custom Animation pane, choose Add Effect, Motion Paths, More Motion Paths, Down. Click and drag the white handle at the end of the path (where the red arrowhead is) to drag it down off the slide. Change the Start setting to With Previous.

TIP

Pressing Shift while you drag an end of a motion path will help you keep the path straight.

---

2. Right-click the downward motion path and choose Reverse Path Direction so that the group looks as if it's entering the slide from the bottom.

3. Select the Financial Services group on the slide and choose Add Effect, Entrance, Fade. Set the Start setting to With Previous. Now the group will fade in as it moves upward onto the slide (see Figure 9.29).

To cover the client logos and make it look as if the Financial Services group is revealing the logos as it wipes up, add a white rectangle to the slide and animate it. To do so, follow these steps:

1. Click the Home tab, go to the Shapes group, and click Rectangle. Click and drag on the slide to create a rectangle that's big enough to cover the logos. On the Drawing Tools Format tab, change the Shape Fill to White, and choose Shape Outline, No Outline. Then click the arrow next to Send to Back and choose Send Backward so that the box doesn't overlap the picture of the woman as it animates.

2. With the white box selected on the slide, choose Add Effect, Exit, More Effects, Wipe. Change the Start setting to With Previous. Drag the animation bar in the Advanced Timeline so that it begins at 1.3 seconds.

TIP

To learn more about the Advanced Timeline, refer to the sidebar "Using the Advanced Animation Timeline," earlier in this chapter.

---

3. Again, with the white box selected on the slide, choose Add Effect, Exit, More Effects, Fade. Change the Start setting to With Previous, and change the Speed setting to Very Fast.

TIP

You can combine two or more animations of the same type to create a new animation. In this instance, we used two exit animations (Wipe and Fade), and then timed them to occur at the same time.

We can call this slide finished, but it would be better to have the Financial Services banner exit off the slide; after all, it sets up a nice transition to the next slide.

1. Select the Financial Services group, and in the Custom Animation pane, choose Add Effect, Motion Paths, More Motion Paths, Down. Click and drag the red handle at the end of the path to drag it down off the slide so that it's the same size as the existing motion path. Change the Start setting to With Previous. Drag the animation effect in the Custom Animation timeline so that it begins at 5 seconds (see Figure 9.30).

2. Select the Financial Services group on the slide, and in the Custom Animation pane, choose Add Effect, Exit, Fade. Change the Start setting to With Previous and the Speed to Fast. Drag the animation bar in the Custom Animation timeline so that it begins at 6 seconds (see Figure 9.30).

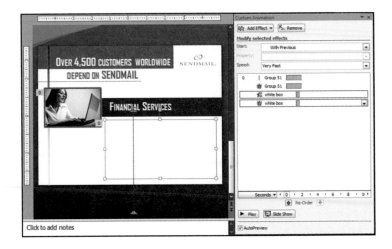

Figure 9.29

This white box will fade and wipe away to reveal the logos underneath. The timing of its exit makes it seem as if the logos appear when the Financial Services banner moves over them.

3. Select the white box on the slide, and in the Custom Animation pane, choose Add Effect, Entrance, Wipe. Change the Start setting to With Previous and the Direction setting to From Top. Drag the animation bar in the Custom Animation timeline so that it begins at 5.4 seconds (see Figure 9.30).

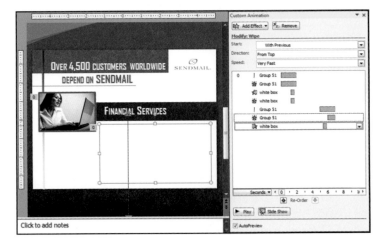

Figure 9.30

The white box uncovers the logos as the banner animates over them. Then it covers them back up as the banner exits the slide. Although we've given you some sample start times, it often takes some trial and error to get it just right.

4. Click the Play button at the bottom of the Custom Animation pane to see what your animation looks like so far. Save your file.

Create a New Slide Based on the Existing Slide

Now that we've completed one customer slide, it will be easy to copy and modify that slide to create another.

If you are following the makeover step by step, continue using your saved presentation. If you just stepped in, you can use the **loop_12.pptx** presentation from the Makeover 08\Steps folder on the CD and continue with these steps.

1. Make a copy of slide 3 by selecting it in the Slides pane, and pressing Ctrl+D. Now, change the Financial Services text to **Retail**.

2. Right-click the picture of the woman and choose Change Picture (see Figure 9.31). This opens the Insert Picture dialog box. Select the picture of the man (7_2502031.jpg in the Makeover 08\Pictures folder on the CD), and click Insert.

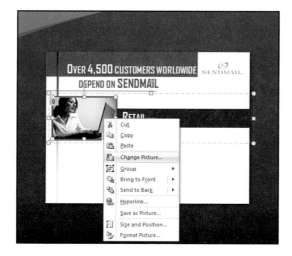

Figure 9.31
PowerPoint 2007 lets you swap pictures with just a right-click! Take advantage of this great new feature.

3. Select the picture of the man on the slide, and on the Picture Tools Format tab, click the Size dialog launcher. Make sure the Lock aspect ratio option is selected; then type **2.75** in the Width box. Drag the picture to the left so that it overlaps the vertical line on the edge of the slide a little.

TIP

A new feature in PowerPoint 2007 is the ability to reposition (and otherwise modify) objects while they're still grouped. This is great because we don't have to ungroup the objects and lose the group's animation settings to edit them.

4. On the Home tab in the Editing group, choose Select, Selection pane. Hide the white box by clicking the eye icon in the Selection and Visibility pane. Now delete the financial services companies' logos and replace them with the retail companies' logos (see Figure 9.32). These logos are in the `Makeover 08\Pictures` folder on the CD.

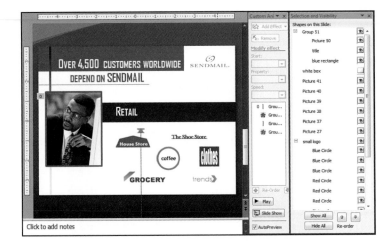

Figure 9.32

Hide the white box using the Selection and Visibility pane so that you can easily work with the items beneath it.

5. Use the Re-Order buttons on the Selection and Visibility pane to move the white box above the logos you just added. Move the Retail group banner so that it is the top layer at the top of the list (see Figure 9.32). You also could use Arrange, Bring to Front on the Home or Drawing Tools Format tabs of the Ribbon. Make the white box visible again by clicking the eye icon.

6. Save your file.

Step 6. Dress Up a Basic Text Slide

Basic text is too boring for a tradeshow loop, so we'll add some punch to these short phrases.

If you are following the makeover step by step, continue using your saved presentation. If you just stepped in, you can use the `loop_13.pptx` presentation from the `Makeover 08\Steps` folder on the CD.

Start with a Copy of an Existing Slide

The objects on slide 2 already are animated, so we can save some time by basing slide 5 on slide 2. Follow these steps:

1. Select slide 2 in the Slides pane, and press Ctrl+D to duplicate the slide. In the Slide pane on the left, drag the duplicated slide to the bottom of the pane, so that this is slide 5.

TIP

You can also right-click the slide in the Slides pane, and choose Duplicate Slide to create a copy of the slide.

---

2. Delete the large logo from the middle of the slide. In addition, delete the red rectangle that extends the entire width of the slide.

3. Type `Email security challenges` in the title placeholder to replace the existing title text. Type `Clogged email systems` in the subtitle placeholder. Select the word "Clogged" and use the Font color tool on the Home tab of the Ribbon to highlight the text by making it red (the Accent 1 color).

4. Move the subtitle placeholder below the horizontal line. Then move the horizontal line below the subtitle placeholder. With the line still selected, drag the end of the line to make it long enough to reach the right edge of the slide. This anchors the text so that it is not floating around in the middle of the slide (see Figure 9.33).

5. If the Custom Animation pane isn't open, click the Animations tab of the Ribbon, and then click Custom Animation. Select the animation effects for the #2 red rectangle, the small logo, the title placeholder, and the blue vertical line in the Custom Animation pane, and delete those animations by right-clicking and selecting Remove.

6. Select the horizontal line on the slide, right-click the motion path, and choose Edit Points. Drag the green arrow end of the motion path so that it extends off the top edge of the slide (see Figure 9.33).

7. In the Custom Animation pane, drag the orange bars for the horizontal line animations to the beginning of the timeline so that there is no delay. Drag or use the Re-Order buttons to move the subtitle animation to the last in the list. (This makes it easier to follow the animation sequence.) Drag the animation bar for the subtitle box so that animation begins at 1.5 seconds (see Figure 9.34).

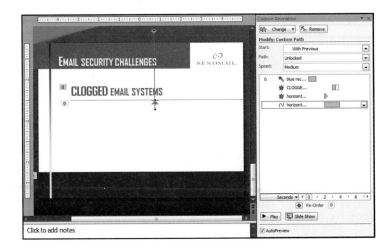

Figure 9.33

Use the Edit Points option to adjust animation motion paths.

Figure 9.34

The Custom Animation pane looks like this after reordering and removing delays from the animations.

Copy and Modify Existing Graphics

Now that you've set up animation for one text and line combination, you can use those as the basis for other text that will animate the same way.

If you are following the makeover step by step, continue using your saved presentation. If you just stepped in, you can use the `loop_14.pptx` presentation from the `Makeover 08\Steps` folder on the CD.

1. Press Shift+click to select the line and subtitle text box. While still pressing Shift, also press Ctrl and drag the line and subtitle text box downward. This creates copies of the objects while keeping them aligned with the originals.

NOTE

The Shift key ensures that dragged objects are moved in 90-degree increments, and the Ctrl key allows you to create copies of dragged objects.

---

2. Change the text to `Vulnerability to attacks`. Adjust the start end of the motion path (refer to step 6 in the previous step sequence) and tweak the animations so that they occur in sequence. Repeat for `Compliance risks` and `Increasing complexity` (see Figure 9.35).

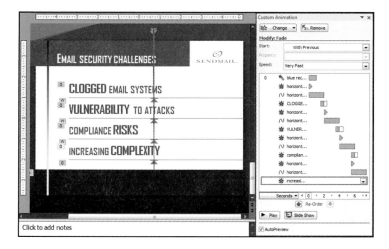

Figure 9.35

If you have repeating elements, add the animation effects for one, and then copy, paste, and change the text for the additional objects. That way, you won't have to redo all the animation effects!

3. Copy the title placeholder and change the text for the tagline to the following: `So, what's your best line of defense?` Shorten the blue rectangle and make it a bit wider so that the text fits inside it. Group the text and rectangle (see Figure 9.36).

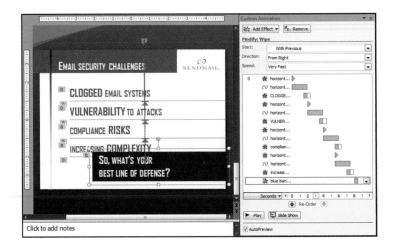

Figure 9.36

This is how the Custom Animation pane and the slide look like after completing all the text and line animations and adding the blue tagline banner.

4. Add a Wipe entrance animation to the blue tagline banner. Change the Start setting to With Previous, the Direction setting to From Right, and the Speed setting to Very Fast. Drag the animation bar so that the animation begins as the animation for the last text box ends (see Figure 9.37). You can rename the group Blue Banner in the Selection pane on the Home tab of the Ribbon to make it easier to see in the Custom Animation pane.

5. Click the Play button at the bottom of the Custom Animation pane to see how your animation looks so far. Save your file.

Add Exit Animations

Because the text on slide 5 has been building, we don't need to leave the tagline visible for too long—a couple seconds is plenty, and then the objects can exit from the slides. To add exit animations, follow these steps.

If you are following the makeover step by step, continue using your saved presentation. If you just stepped in, you can use the `loop_15.pptx` presentation from the `Makeover 08\Steps` folder on the CD.

1. Select the red rectangle on the slide on slide 5, and apply a Fly Out exit animation. Change the Start setting to With Previous and the Speed setting to Fast. Drag the animation bar so that this animation begins about 2 seconds after the previous animation ends, at about 10.5 seconds (see Figure 9.37).

0

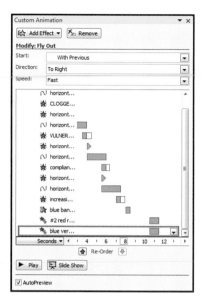

Figure 9.37

These exit animations begin a couple seconds after the previous animations end. Delays are indicated by gaps in the advanced timeline.

2. Select the vertical line on the slide and apply a Fly Out exit animation. Change the Start setting to With Previous, the Direction setting to To Right, and the Speed setting to Fast (see Figure 9.37).

3. Select the blue tagline banner on the slide, and apply an Up motion path animation. Click and drag the stop (red) end of the motion path upward toward the top of the slide to adjust the end position of the animation. Press the Shift key while you do this to keep the path vertical. Change the Start setting to With Previous and the Speed setting to Fast.

4. Add a rectangle to the slide, and then give it a white fill color and no outline using the tools on the Drawing Tools Format tab of the Ribbon. Apply a Wipe entrance animation, and then change the Start setting to With Previous, the Direction setting to From Left, and the Speed setting to Fast. Adjust its size and position so that it covers the four text boxes (see Figure 9.38).

5. Click the Home tab, and in the Editing group, choose Select, Selection Pane. Name the rectangle you drew in the previous step `white box`. Use the Re-Order buttons to rearrange the objects so that they appear in this order: blue banner, blue vertical line, title, #2 red rectangle, white box. This ensures that the white rectangle appears below the exiting objects—but still above the text boxes it's supposed to cover (see Figure 9.38).

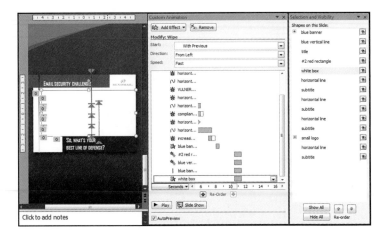

Figure 9.38
After animating and reordering, this is what the slide, Custom Animation pane, and Selection pane should look like.

6. Click the Play button at the bottom of the Custom Animation pane to see how your animation looks so far. Save your file.

Step 7. Add a Picture of the Product

The final slide in the draft presentation encourages people to transform the way they network by using Sendmail Sentrion. Showing a picture of the product is more interesting than just displaying some text.

If you are following the makeover step by step, continue using your saved presentation. If you just stepped in, you can use the **loop_16.pptx** presentation from the Makeover 08\Steps folder on the CD.

Start with a Copy of an Existing Slide

The objects on slide 5 are animated, so we can save some time by basing slide 6 on slide 5. Follow these steps:

1. Select slide 5 in the Slides pane, and press Ctrl+D to duplicate the slide.

2. Delete the white box, the four text boxes, and the lines from the slide.

3. Remove the animation from the blue banner and position the banner where its animation ends. To do this, click the Drawing Tools Format tab, and then click the Size group dialog launcher. On the Position tab, change the Vertical setting to **1.3"**.

TIP

It's difficult to determine the endpoint of an object's motion path animation. The free Motion Path Tools add-in from Microsoft PowerPoint MVP Shyam Pillai will help you overcome this limitation of PowerPoint. Download it from http://skp.mvps.org/mptools.htm.

4. Change the text in the title placeholder to `Transform the way you protect your email network`, and add the text `with Sendmail Sentrion` in the subtitle placeholder. (You might need to resize the font in the subtitle placeholder to 42 pt.) Press Shift+Enter to add a line break between the words "you" and "email" in the title placeholder.

5. Increase the height of the red rectangle to 1.58" to match the height of the blue rectangle. Align the two rectangles and text boxes (see Figure 9.39). Drag the red rectangle so it spans the width of the slide.

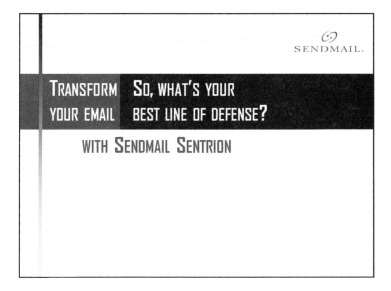

Figure 9.39

Align the text boxes and rectangles before moving the blue banner behind the red one.

Add Animation

Now we can add some animation to the text and objects we just created. Follow these steps:

1. Right-click the red rectangle's animation in the Custom Animation pane, and click Remove to remove the exit animation. Select the red rectangle on the slide and click Add Effect, Entrance, Wipe to add a wipe animation. Specify Start With Previous, Direction From Left, and Speed Fast. Drag the animation effect bar to the beginning of the timeline so it begins at 0.0 seconds.

2. The blue vertical line exited from the previous slide, so we'll make it enter onto this slide from the same side. Select the Vertical Line animation effect in the Custom Animation pane. Click the Change button, and then choose Entrance, More Effects, Fly In. Change the Start setting to With Previous, the Direction setting to From Right, and the Speed setting to Fast. Drag the animation bar to the beginning of the timeline so it also begins at 0.0 seconds.

3. Select the title placeholder ("Transform…") and apply a Fade entrance animation. Specify the Start setting as With Previous and the Speed setting as Very Fast. Double-click the effect to open the Fade effect options dialog box and choose to Animate Text By Letter. Type **5** for the percent delay between letters. Drag the animation bar so that this animation begins at 1.0 seconds, when the previous animations end. Repeat this step for the subtitle placeholder, dragging it to a start time of 2.0 seconds (see Figure 9.40).

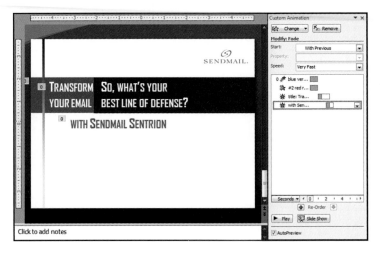

Figure 9.40

Add animations to the objects on the slide. The white bars appended to the orange animation bars indicate "by letter" text animations.

4. Add the product picture to the slide by clicking the Insert tab on the Ribbon, then Picture, and choosing `sentrion.png` on the `Makeover 08\Pictures` folder on the CD. Apply a Wipe entrance animation. Set the Start setting to With Previous and the Speed setting to Fast. Drag the picture to the lower-right corner of the slide.

5. Select the blue vertical line, title, and subtitle placeholders, and drag them to the right until the line touches the edge of the photo.

6. Use the Selection and Visibility pane to move the blue banner behind the red rectangle and the picture below the vertical line (see Figure 9.41).

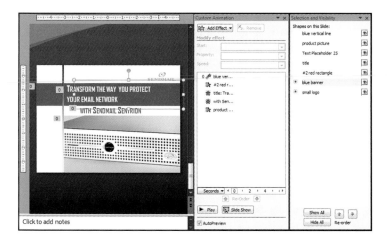

Figure 9.41

Use the Selection and Visibility pane to move objects above or beneath other objects.

Now we want to apply exit animations to all objects to return to a blank white slide. To do so, follow these steps:

1. Select the blue banner and apply a Disappear exit animation. Set the Start setting to With Previous, and drag the effect so that it begins about 2 seconds after the previous animation ends (around 5.2 seconds).

2. For the remaining exit animations, set the Start setting to With Previous and the Speed setting to Fast.

   ■ For the red rectangle, use Fly Out with a Direction setting of To Right.

   ■ For the blue vertical line, use Fly Out with a Direction setting of To Left.

   ■ For the picture, use Wipe with a Direction setting of From Top.

   ■ For the logo, use Fade.

   We want the subtitle placeholder to exit the opposite of its entrance animation, so use Fade with Speed set to Very Fast. Double-click to open the Effect Options, choose Animate Text By Letter, and type **5** for the percent delay between letters (see Figure 9.42)

3. Click the Play button at the bottom of the Custom Animation pane to see how your animation looks so far. Save your file.

Figure 9.42

This shows the animation sequence for slide 6.

Step 8. Create an End Slide to Close the Loop

Because we want our tradeshow loop to actually look like a loop, we'll copy slide 1 and paste it to use as the basis for our last slide.

If you are following the makeover step by step, continue using your saved presentation. If you just stepped in, you can use the `loop_17.pptx` presentation from the `Makeover 08\Steps` folder on the CD.

In the Slides pane, select slide 1 and press Ctrl+D to duplicate it; then follow these steps:

  1. Drag the duplicate slide so it's the last one in the Slides pane.

  2. Delete the logo, including the text part of the logo and the six small circles.

  3. Add Wipe entrance animations to both the red and blue rectangles. Set the Start setting to With Previous and the Speed setting to Fast. The Direction should be From Right for the red and From Left for the blue.

Now set the slide transitions so that the presentation moves automatically from one slide to the next. To do so, follow these steps:

  1. Click the Animations tab, and click Custom Animation to open the pane, if it's not already open. Right-click in the pane and choose Show Advanced Timeline.

2. Starting with slide 1, scroll to the bottom of the Custom Animation pane and hover over the last animation to see how long the animation takes to complete.

3. Using the animation time as a rough guide, input appropriate slide transition times in the Automatically After box on the Animations tab of the Ribbon (see Figure 9.43). We used the following times:

- slide 1, 00:06
- slide 2, 00:04.5
- slide 3, 00:07
- slide 4, 00:07
- slide 5, 00:12
- slide 6, 00:06.5
- slide 7, 00:01

Figure 9.43

Specify automatic transition timings for slides on the Animations pane.

4. Finally, click the Slide Show tab, and then click Set Up Slide Show to open the Set Up Show dialog box. Check the Loop Continuously Until 'Esc' option so that the presentation will play in a continuous loop.

5. Save your file.

Step 9. Add Music

Background music is good to include on standalone presentations. PowerPoint can't perfectly synchronize animations or slide transitions with music, but it does a good job playing a background track.

IndigoRose provided the background music file for this makeover. You can find more royalty free music on the CD.

If you are following the makeover step by step, continue using your saved presentation. If you just stepped in, you can use the **loop_18.pptx** presentation from the Makeover 08\Steps folder on the CD.

To add music to the presentation, follow these steps:

1. Copy the `HaveMercy.mp3` file from the `Makeover 08\Steps` folder on the CD to the same folder as your open presentation.

TIP

Before you insert any sound or movie files within your presentation, copy the media files to the same folder as the presentation so that PowerPoint can remember where the file is located. This is especially important if your media files are on a CD, thumb drive, network folder, or external hard disk. Even if the media files are located in the same computer as the presentation, it's a good idea to copy them to the same folder in case you want to share the presentation. Then, all you will need to do is copy the whole folder to share your presentation—this also ensures that the sounds and movies will work everywhere without broken links.

---

2. On slide 1, click the Insert tab, click the arrow beneath the Sound icon, click Sound From File, choose the `HaveMercyMedium.mp3` file that you copied in the previous step, and click OK.

CAUTION

The only sound file that can be *embedded* into PowerPoint is a WAV file. Before you insert a WAV into your presentation, click Office Button, PowerPoint Options, Advanced, and then input **50000** in the Link Sounds with File Size Greater Than box to embed WAVs nearly 50MB in size.

All other sound file types are linked. (For example, the MP3 music we just added to our presentation will be linked.) To help keep the links intact, copy the sound files into the same folder with your presentation before inserting them. In addition, be sure to include both the PowerPoint file and the sounds if you move the presentation to another computer!

---

3. PowerPoint opens a message box asking if you want to play the sound Automatically or When Clicked. Choose Automatically (see Figure 9.44).

Figure 9.44

When you insert sounds, PowerPoint prompts you to choose to play them automatically or when clicked.

4. Select the sound icon on the slide, and then click the Sound Tools Options tab. Choose Loop Until Stopped, and then choose Play Sound: Play Across Slides. You also can click Hide During Show (see Figure 9.45), or you can drag the icon off the edge of the slide so that it doesn't show during the presentation.

Figure 9.45

Make the sound play across slides by choosing that setting on the Sound Tools Options tab of the Ribbon.

5. Click the Animations tab, and click Custom Animation to open the pane, if it's not already open. You will see the sound animation at the bottom of the Custom Animation pane. Drag it to the top (see Figure 9.46).

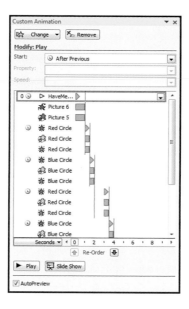

Figure 9.46

Drag the sound's animation effect so that it appears first in the list of animations.

6. Play the show to see it in all its glory, and be sure to turn up the speakers! To play the slide show full-screen, press F5 on your keyboard or click the Slide Show tab on the Ribbon and choose From Beginning. You also can click the Slide Show button on the Custom Animation pane or click the Slide Show icon on the Status bar.

You can play the completed presentation by opening the `loop_19.pptx` presentation from the `Makeover 08\Steps` folder on the CD.

Resources

10

The Gallery

This chapter is more about pictures than words. We use visual content to show you what works better, and in most examples, we show you the "before" and "after" stages as well.

Color Coordination

Remember that the backgrounds in a slide must remain in the background! It's easy to forget this when you use backgrounds composed of colors that are highly saturated and bright. True, these may look great as wallpapers, but if you allow the background to scream, it's going to take attention away from everything else, including the subject of your presentation.

Choose Themes Wisely

Slide A in Figure 10.1 uses one of PowerPoint's built-in theme color sets, but it certainly is a wrong choice. The background and foreground colors are both highly saturated values, and the slide seems to be screaming more than anything else.

In contrast, slide B uses subtle and less-saturated colors that do not take attention from the real content on the slide. Moreover, these colors will project well.

- Make Good Design Choices
- Use Fonts, Pictures, and Shapes Successfully
- Create Harmonious Color Selections

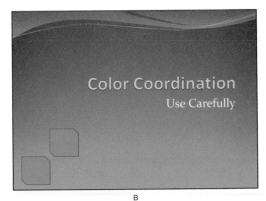

A   B

Figure 10.1

Pay attention to how your content is affected by your choice of theme or background.

Consider Color When Using Text Effects

Beveled text with drop shadows does not work with all colors. The color set shown on slide A in Figure 10.2 is quite nice, but it cannot cope well with a large, empty expanse and text with drop shadows.

On the other hand, slide B uses one subtle color (for the background) and one bright color (for the text). This works well and can cope with all sorts of effects that PowerPoint 2007 allows, such as drop shadows and beveled text.

A   B

Figure 10.2

Text effects often work better against subtle backgrounds.

Consider Changing Theme Colors

Both slides in Figure 10.3 use PowerPoint's built-in theme colors, and that shows how important it is to experiment with the choices that are available.

Slide A uses the default colors associated with the theme. This isn't too bad, but we won't call this professional. The gray and pink seem to be at war.

On slide B, blue and yellow seem to be happier, and they provide a more pleasing balance.

You can learn more about Theme Color sets and how to create and apply them in Chapter 6, "Makeover 5: Halloween Scrapbook."

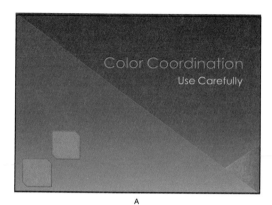
A

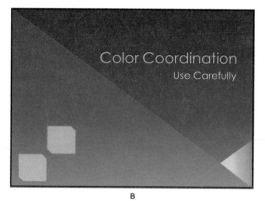
B

Figure 10.3

It's fun to play around applying Theme Color sets, and it can be rewarding as well.

Avoid Clashing Colors That Sacrifice Contrast

The brown used on slide A in Figure 10.4 is too saturated, and the blue is too bright. It's almost as if the colors are opposing each other. The gray seen on slide B is perfect as a neutral color, and a more subdued blue makes this a winner.

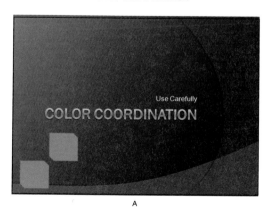
A

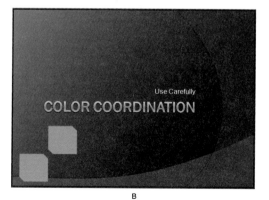
B

Figure 10.4

A little variation in color can bring harmony and coexistence.

Text Contrast

Whatever you do, make sure that your text can be read. In addition, make sure that your text is not in some teeny-weeny font size that makes the audience squint their eyes, then feel tired, then sleep, and finally snore!

Speaking of contrast, remember that your text color should not be similar to the background color. The sections that follow explain more.

Examine Theme Text Colors

This slide (see Figure 10.5) is based on one of PowerPoint 2007's built-in themes. The backdrop is beautiful, but you need to be careful with the text colors. Dark text works well, but text that is lighter than, or even similar to, the background colors does not make any impact.

Figure 10.5
Be sure your text contrasts with the background so it can be read.

Contrasting Colors

Both slides shown in Figure 10.6 use a plain color background. Slide A has a dark (black) background while slide B has a light (white) background. As expected, colors contrasting with the backgrounds work best.

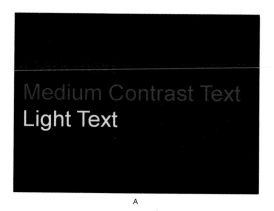

Figure 10.6
Use dark text on a light background, and vice versa.

Contrast in Gradients

Gradient backgrounds can be tough when it comes to creating contrast. This slide (see Figure 10.7) uses a gradient background that includes both dark and light areas. If you use a slide like this, you need to make sure that the text color contrasts in both the dark and light areas. As you can see, the light text in the lower area of the slide is clearly visible, but text in the same color might be illegible in the top area of the slide.

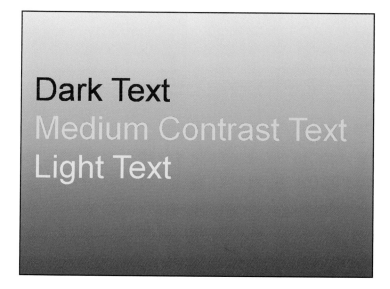

Figure 10.7
It's especially important to check text for readability on both light and dark areas of gradient backgrounds.

Text and Pictures

Picture backgrounds are not too compatible with text because pictures typically contain a riot of colors in different hues and saturation values. If your text is a light color, insert a shape in a dark color behind the text, and make the shape semitransparent, as you can see in slide B. On the other hand, if your text needs to be in a dark color, insert a shape in a light color (see slide C).

A

B

C

Figure 10.8
Semitransparent shapes can help make text more visible on busy backgrounds.

Shape Styles Gallery

The Shape Styles gallery is quite addictive and can provide umpteen hours of fun if you start playing with all the options! However, that might actually be time well spent.

All the fills, outlines, and effects for the shapes in the Shape Styles gallery actually come from the active theme of the presentation, including the Theme Effects and Theme Colors. This means that when you can change the theme of the presentation, all the shapes in your presentation that have shape styles applied to them get changed to the colors and effects in the new theme. Not only is this almost magical, but also it ensures that your presentation always uses the right colors for all elements.

The four slides in Figures 10.9 through 10.12 include the same shapes with different themes applied. As you can see, the Shape Styles updated themselves successfully each time.

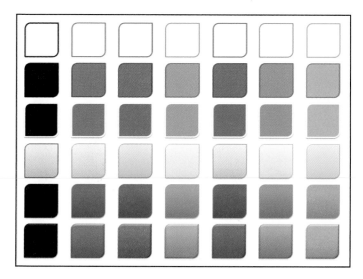

Figure 10.9
Theme: Office.

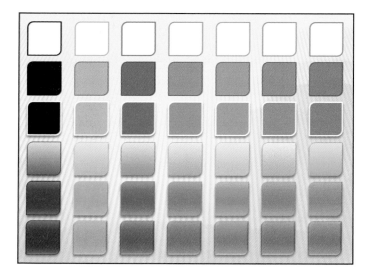

Figure 10.10
Theme: Trek.

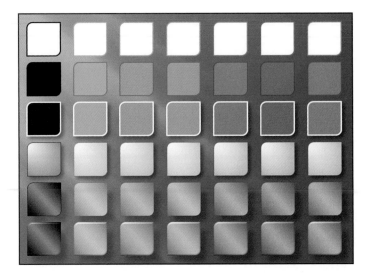

Figure 10.11
Theme: Apex.

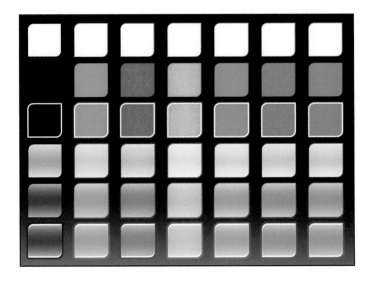

Figure 10.12
Theme: Metro.

Picture Styles

It's surprisingly easy to add drop shadows, bevels, borders, and other niceties to pictures on PowerPoint slides by using the Picture Effects engine built in to PowerPoint. Although it is easy to apply, let me tell you what makes it even easier: the new Picture Styles drop-down gallery in the Picture Tools Format tab of the Ribbon.

See the Picture Styles options shown in Figures 10.13 through 10.16.

Figure 10.13

Effects (clockwise from top left): Reflected Rounded Rectangle; Reflected Bevel, Black; Metal Rounded Rectangle; Perspective Shadow, White.

Figure 10.14

Effects (clockwise from top left): Rounded Diagonal Corner, White; Snip Diagonal Corner, White; Rotated, White; Reflected Bevel, White.

Figure 10.15

Effects (clockwise from top left): Bevel Rectangle; Bevel Perspective Left, White; Relaxed Perspective, White; Reflected Perspective, White.

Figure 10.16

Effects (clockwise from top left): Metal Frame; Metal Oval; Bevel Perspective; Simple Frame, Black.

Don't Use These Fonts

Well, we're not really going to ask you to stay away from any particular font style, but we do have some opinions that we want to share.

Avoid Using Too Many Font Styles in a Presentation

Some PowerPoint users want to type every line of their presentation in a different font style. While we don't want to curtail their freedom, they should know that's the very reason why Microsoft introduced the Theme Fonts option in this version of PowerPoint. See Figure 10.17 for an example that speaks louder than words or fonts!

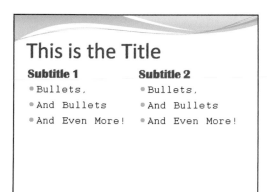 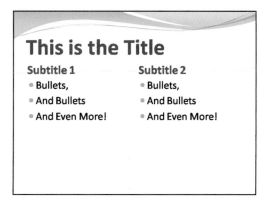

Figure 10.17

Try using variations in normal, bold, color, and italics within the same font style rather than using different fonts.

Use Suitable Fonts

Many fonts look a little edgy, and while they are great for an invitation to an exhibition of contemporary art, a fashion catalog, or even a wedding card, they won't exactly work in a presentation scenario.

For the same reason, stay away from script style fonts, especially, because they are so hard to read! (See Figure 10.18.)

TIP

The font used for the main title in Figure 10.18 is known as a *display* font. Although display fonts can be useful for small bits of text, they're not usually good to use for slide titles and body text because they're so decorative.

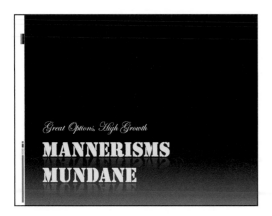
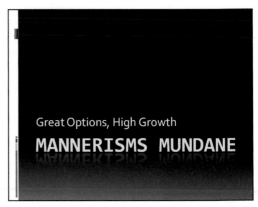

Figure 10.18

Script style fonts can look elegant, but you cannot compromise on readability. In addition, the font for the main title is not a script, and it's too blocky. It looks huge and uses two lines of space rather than one.

Use Caution with Dingbats

Dingbats are those cute fonts that produce drawings and illustrations rather than actual alphabet characters. Many people love to use them as bullets, but when these presentations travel to another computer where the dingbat font is not installed, they end up showing as ugly boxes, as you can see in Figure 10.19. Even if you embed the fonts while saving the presentation, anything used as a bullet does not get embedded, so be careful with this one.

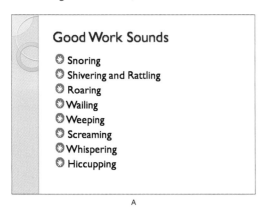
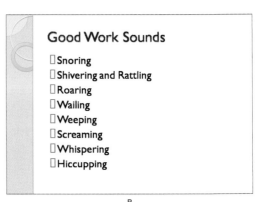

A   B

Figure 10.19

Dingbat bullets don't travel well.

Color Harmonies

Color harmonies are a difficult subject, and we really can't cover it in a page or two; it needs an entire book. However, we'll make it as easy as we can for you.

TIP

For most purposes, you need not learn more than what we explain in this section, but if you do want to learn more, please do so because it will make your presentations look so much more professional.

You'll find links to some online resources on this book's companion site: http://www.pptkit.com/color/.

Based on the colors in the harmonies, you can create your own Theme Color sets. Use the background color of the slide as a starting point, and use the color harmonies to find hues that will work well with that particular background color.

There are several types of color harmonies, but four of them work best in PowerPoint. We'll explain to you how these work using the simple color wheel that you see in Figure 10.20.

Figure 10.20
The basic color wheel shows all the colors in one circle.

Monochromatic

A monochromatic color harmony uses different hues of the same color to create an elegant look (see Figure 10.21). Monochromatic harmonies are successful almost all the time, but they can look a little dull.

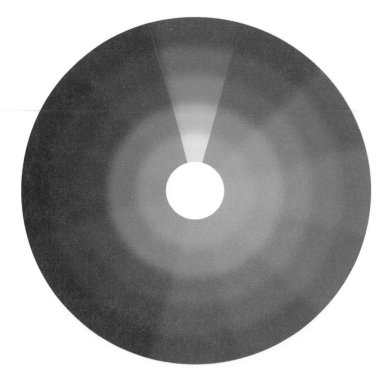

Figure 10.21

If the color wheel were a pie chart, monochromatic colors would be found within a thin slice of the pie. We isolated the blue family in this color wheel to show you how this works.

Analogous

Analogous harmonies use similar color values. They build on the monochromatic choices, and you can extend that a little more so that you get a larger range of choices in the pie slice, as you can see in Figure 10.22. Thus, if you start with blue-green, you also could delve into any blue or green shade.

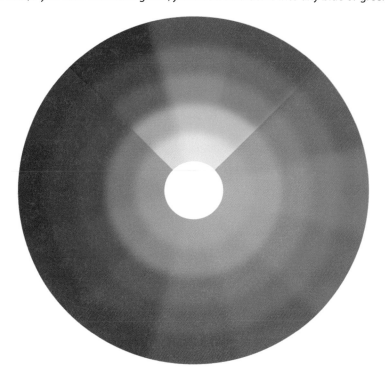

Figure 10.22

Continuing with our pie chart concept, you can see that the pie slice is three times larger for the analogous harmonies, as compared to the monochromatic ones.

Split Complementary

Split complementary harmonies provide a much larger choice of colors, but those are mainly in the opposite side of the wheel, as you can see in Figure 10.23.

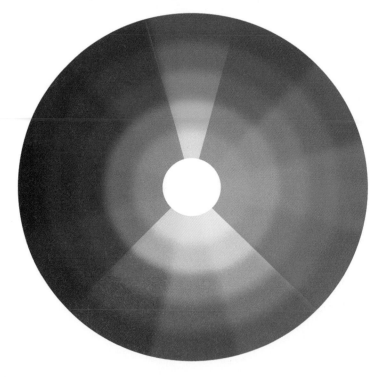

Figure 10.23
Like analogous, split complementary harmonies extend the size of the pie. Unlike analogous, they do so in the opposite side of the color wheel.

Double Complementary

Double complementary harmonies take a different approach. They place a rectangle over the color wheel, and each of the four corners of this rectangle comprises the areas from which colors can be sourced for this color harmony, as you can see in Figure 10.24.

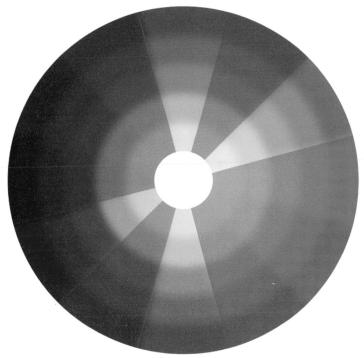

Figure 10.24

Double complementary harmonies use colors that are entirely different from each other.

On the CD

Makeover Files

The following is the folder structure where you will find the source files for following the makeovers in this book:

- Makeover 01\Steps
- Makeover 01\Pictures
- Makeover 02\Steps
- Makeover 02\Theme
- Makeover 03\Steps
- Makeover 03\Pictures
- Makeover 04\Steps
- Makeover 05\Steps
- Makeover 05\Pictures
- Makeover 06\Steps
- Makeover 06\Pictures
- Makeover 07\Steps
- Makeover 07\Pictures
- Makeover 08\Steps
- Makeover 08\Theme
- Makeover 08\Pictures

Utilities and Supporting Applications

The following list of utilities and supporting applications have been included to provide you with additional resources for creating your own PowerPoint makeovers:

- **PhotoSpin Images**—PhotoSpin has graciously provided 25 pictures. You'll find many of these pictures as files to use in the PowerPoint makeovers, and the remaining pictures are in the Media\PhotoSpin folder.

- **Ppted Templates**—Ppted.com has provided five sets of five PowerPoint templates each from its designer collections. This is worth $100.

- **PowerFrameworks Sampler**—PowerFrameworks has provided a substantial sampler of its readymade frameworks that you can use in your PowerPoint presentations.

- **Pictures from Geetesh**—Several pictures from Geetesh's own collection.

- **TechSmith Demos**—Demo versions of TechSmith SnagIt and TechSmith Camtasia Studio.

- **Opuzz Sampler**—A music sampler from Opuzz.

- **IndigoRose Music Clips**—Sample clips from the Liquid Cabaret collection are included as part of the files for Makeover 08.

- **Sample SmartArt Chapter**—A PDF of the SmartArt chapter from Geetesh's other book, *Special Edition Using Microsoft Office PowerPoint 2007*, also published by Que.

- **RnR PPTools Starter Set**—A free add-in that includes a collection of handy tools to help you quickly hammer images into place, change font sizes by 1-point increments, and more. Demo versions of other RnR add-ins are also included.

- **Plays for Certain Media Tools**—Demo versions of PFCMedia and PFCPro to help you insert video and DVD into PowerPoint and make sure it "plays for certain."

- **Ribbon Customizer**—This demo version of Ribbon Customizer Professional lets you customize the Ribbon to your heart's content!

You will find Chapter 11 here as well.

Index

A

Advanced Timeline (Custom Animation pane), 172, 179

aligning

  logos, tradeshow presentations, 167-168

  placeholders in slide layouts, 25

  shapes, 88

  tabs in slides, 46-47

analogous color harmonies, 221

anchoring text to placeholders, 41-43

animation

  Custom Animation pane

    Advanced Timeline, 172, 179

    Show Advanced Timeline, 172

    Timing tab, 174

  customer lists, adding to tradeshow presentations, 186-187

  exit animations

    adding to text slides, 194-195

    Kiosk presentations, 144

  logos, adding to tradeshow presentations, 168-174

  message slides, adding to, 177-184

  pictures, adding to tradeshow presentations, 197-199

  schemes, 17

  slides, adding to tradeshow presentations, 177-184

  timing, 174

  trigger animations, Kiosk presentations, 141-144

aspect ratios, tradeshow presentations, 165

audio, adding to tradeshow presentations, 201-203

autofitting (text), turning on/off, 34-35

Awards slide, Kiosk presentations, 145

B

backgrounds (slides)

  Halloween scrapbook presentations, changing in, 94-97

  Hide Background Graphics option, 98

C

D - E

F

G

M

N

O - P

Q - R

S

U - V - W

X - Y - Z